Taxing the Family

A Conference Sponsored by the
American Enterprise Institute for Public Policy Research

Taxing the Family

Edited by Rudolph G. Penner

American Enterprise Institute for Public Policy Research
Washington and London

I would like to thank Cheryl Janas, Dennis Brent Melby, Arthur Upshur, and Kathy Ormiston for their valuable assistance in completing this volume.

343.7305
T19
125-976
aug. 1983

R.G.P.

Library of Congress Cataloging in Publication Data
Main entry under title:

Taxing the family.

(AEI symposia ; 83A)
Proceedings of a conference sponsored by the American Enterprise Institute, held Oct. 13, 1981.
1. Income tax—Law and legislation—United States—Congresses. 2. Family—Taxation—Law and legislation—United States—Congresses. 3. Social security—Law and legislation—United States—Congresses. I. Penner, Rudolph Gerhard, 1936–   II. American Enterprise Institute for Public Policy Research. III. Series.
KF6369.A2T33   1983   343.7305′2   83–9929
ISBN 0–8447–2244–8   347.30352
ISBN 0–8447–2243–X (pbk.)

AEI Symposia 83A

1 3 5 7 9 10 8 6 4 2

Printed in the United States of America

Participants

Gerard Brannon
Director of Special Projects, Taxes, Pensions, and Welfare
American Council of Life Insurance

Geoffrey Brennan
Professor of Economics
Center for Public Choice
Virginia Polytechnic Institute and State University

Richard V. Burkhauser
Assistant Professor of Economics
Vanderbilt University

Edwin Cohen
Partner, Law Firm of Covington and Burling

Bruce Davie
Professional Assistant
House Ways and Means Committee

Daniel Feenberg
Research Associate
National Bureau of Economic Research

Charles Gustafson
Associate Professor of Law
Georgetown University Law Center

Ronald Hoffman
Senior Economist
Office of Special Studies
U.S. Department of the Treasury

Thomas Johnson
Director of Economic Policy Studies
American Enterprise Institute

Mickey Levy
Research Associate
American Enterprise Institute

Michael McIntyre
Professor of Law
Wayne State University Law School

Peter Mieszkowski
Allyn R. and Gladys M. Cline Professor of Economics and Finance
Rice University

Joseph J. Minarik
Deputy Assistant Director
Tax Analysis Division
Congressional Budget Office

June O'Neill
Director, Program of Research on Women and the Family
The Urban Institute

Joseph Pechman
Director of Economic Studies
Brookings Institution

Rudolph G. Penner
Director of Fiscal Policy Studies
American Enterprise Institute

Virginia P. Reno
Acting Director, Program Analysis Staff
Social Security Administration

Bernard Saffran
Professor of Economics
Swarthmore College

Bert Seidman
Director, Social Security Department, AFL-CIO

Carl Shoup
Emeritus Professor of Economics
Columbia University

John Shoven
Professor of Economics
Stanford University

Eugene Steuerle
Economist, Tax Analysis Division
U.S. Department of the Treasury

Lawrence Thompson
Director, Office of Research and Statistics
Social Security Administration

Melinda M. Upp
Analyst, Program Analysis Staff
Social Security Administration

Richard Wagner
Professor of Economics and Policy Sciences
Florida State University

*This conference was held at
the American Enterprise Institute
in Washington, D.C., on October 13, 1981.*

Contents

Foreword

Recent changes in the nature of family relationships suggest that many tax and social security laws, enacted before two-income marriages and divorce became as common as they are today, now have unintended consequences. These issues were explored in a one-day conference on "Taxing the Family," held on October 13, 1981, at the American Enterprise Institute. This volume contains the proceedings of that conference.

June O'Neill describes the origins of the so-called marriage penalty whereby two-earner couples can have a higher tax burden than if each earned the same income as a single individual. She argues that husbands and wives should file separately as in many European countries and states of the United States. Many commentators, however, thought this would create administrative problems in the United States.

Daniel Feenberg discusses the attempt of 1981 legislation to mitigate the marriage penalty and estimates that the legislation should encourage the work effort of married women sufficiently to recoup about one-third of the revenues that would be lost if there were no labor supply response. He also examines the effects of the child care credit. Since it is more beneficial to low- than to high-income parents, the child care credit has the effect of increasing marginal tax rates. Consequently, it turns out to be a tax reduction that actually reduces work effort.

Eugene Steuerle investigates change in the tax treatment of families of different size. He shows that since World War II the large family has received relatively less and less of a tax advantage, largely because percentage increases in the basic exemption for dependents have fallen far short of increases in personal income. He discusses various criteria that could be used to determine the tax treatment of large versus small families, but his main point is that dramatic changes in taxing the family have occurred over time without any public debate.

Geoffrey Brennan examines the equity implications of estate taxation and concludes that it is very difficult to rationalize under any of the criteria of equity usually used by public finance scholars. This conclusion provoked a lively debate, with many discussants believing there is a rationale for taxing large bequests to individuals who did little to earn them.

Virginia Reno and Melinda Upp investigated biases in the social security system against working wives and in favor of homemakers. They concluded that it is very difficult to come up with a system that deals adequately with working wives, divorcées, and the disabled. They favor incremental reforms over comprehensive reforms because the latter are very likely to have unintended consequences.

All the papers stimulated lively discussion, though it cannot be claimed that any issues were definitively resolved. In a rapidly changing social and economic environment, however, appropriate public policies toward the family are not sufficiently debated in a rational and unemotional manner. It was AEI's goal to provide a forum for such a debate, and in this I believe we have succeeded.

WILLIAM J. BAROODY, JR.
President
American Enterprise Institute

Taxing the Family

A Conference Sponsored by the
American Enterprise Institute for Public Policy Research

Family Issues in Taxation

June O'Neill

A basic problem in designing a tax system or an income transfer program is determining the appropriate unit of account. The individual may be treated as a separate entity whose taxpaying ability (or benefit needs) is based solely on his own identifiable income-producing capacity. Alternatively, family interdependence and responsibilities may be taken into account.

Before 1948, the U.S. personal income tax focused on the individual by taxing each person's "entire net income received" according to the same rate schedule.[1] Individual income taxation is practiced in many developed countries—for example, fourteen of the twenty-four countries of the Organization for Economic Cooperation and Development (OECD) allow or require it.[2] As a result of the Revenue Act of 1948 and several subsequent embellishments, however, the current U.S. federal tax law bases taxpaying ability on marital and family affiliations. The U.S. social security system taxes individuals according to their own earnings in covered employment, but bases the benefit structure on the family unit.

In recent years the treatment of the family in both the income tax system and the social security system has come under increasingly sharp attack. One reason for the growing criticism is the shift in the social and demographic make-up of the taxpaying population. The once dominant husband-wife family in which the husband is the sole provider of money income has declined in importance, while the two-earner family, the single-parent family, and the single-person household have become relatively more numerous. In 1960, families in which the husband was the sole earner accounted for 34 percent of all U.S. households; in 1979 they accounted for only 16 percent of all households (table 1). The growing numbers of two-earner couples and nonmarried individuals protest that they pay more than their fair share in a tax and benefit structure that subsidizes the married person with a "dependent" spouse. Moreover, the implication that wives are dependents, which underlies

1

TABLE 1

CHANGES IN THE COMPOSITION OF AMERICAN HOUSEHOLDS, 1950–1979
(percent)

	1950	1960	1970	1979
All households (thousands)	43,554	52,799	63,401	77,330
Families	89.2	85.0	81.2	74.4
Husband-wife	78.2	74.3	70.5	61.6
Earnings status: [a]				
Husband-wife earn	19.6	25.6	32.3	31.3
Husband only earns	{ 58.6 }	34.2	24.1	15.8
Other combinations [b]		14.5	14.2	14.5
Other male-headed	2.7	2.3	1.9	2.1
Female-headed	8.3	8.4	8.7	10.6
Nonfamily households [c]	10.8	15.0	18.8	25.6
Persons living alone	10.8	13.4	17.5	22.2
Total (all households)	100.0	100.0	100.0	100.0

a. Based on receipt of earnings in the preceding year.

b. Includes no-earner couples, and couples where the husband and other family members but not the wife are earners, and couples where the wife but not the husband earns.

c. Includes unrelated individuals living together, not shown separately.

SOURCES: Number of families and households, by type: *Statistical Abstract of the United States,* 1979, p. 46, and 1980, pp. 44-45; earnings status: 1950 is based on the percentage of married women in the labor force adjusted to an earnings basis by the ratio of earnings to labor force participation in other years (data from *Employment and Training Report of the President*); 1960 Current Population Report, P-23, no. 39; 1970 and 1979: U.S. Bureau of Labor Statistics, *Marital and Family Characteristics of the Labor Force,* March 1979 (Special Labor Force Report 237, table 1).

many of the income and social security provisions, is viewed by many as objectionable in a world where the role of women is rapidly changing.

The changing composition of households has probably altered the political climate. At the same time, developments in economic theory and in empirical research have enhanced our understanding of issues such as the allocation of time between market and nonmarket activities, the division of labor within the family, and the determinants of money income. These areas are relevant to any evaluation of the tax treatment of the family. This paper attempts to apply some of these new insights to the old criteria by which the current tax treatment of the family is typically evaluated: Is it fair? Is it efficient? Are we making the proper trade-off between fairness and efficiency?

The next section looks at the historical development of the changing tax unit in the personal income tax and then discusses the effect of nonmarket work and labor supply factors on the equity and efficiency criteria by which the appropriate tax unit is determined. Finally, the treatment of the "dependent" spouse in social security is examined, taking into account similar criteria.

The Individual Income Tax

Change in the Tax Unit over Time. Between 1913, when the taxation of personal income first began in the United States, and 1948, all individuals were taxed on the same progressive rate schedule, regardless of marital status. Because of the progressivity in the schedule it was advantageous for a taxpayer to shift a portion of his income to a spouse with little or no money income, since the tax on two lower-income components would be less than the tax on the whole income. For taxpayers in common law states this could only be done if property rights were legally transferred to another family member. Moreover, the splitting of earned income, even if backed by a contractual agreement between husband and wife, was specifically barred in 1930 by the U.S. Supreme Court in *Lucas* v. *Earl*, which asserted that salaries could only be taxed to those who earned them. As a major exception, married taxpayers in community property states were allowed to split their incomes because in these states the law vests in each spouse half of the couple's combined income.[3]

The different treatment of taxpayers according to state of residence became a major issue in the 1940s when income tax rates and coverage were greatly increased to pay for World War II. During the late 1940s when the issue became intense, close to 80 percent of households consisted of husband-wife families, and in only 20 percent of these families did the wife have earnings. Thus, the vast majority of the taxpaying population faced a substantial tax reduction under income splitting. Congress could have passed legislation requiring that each married person pay tax on his or her own income, thereby superseding community property laws.[4] The composition of the taxpaying public, however, would have made such a move politically improbable.

In 1948, the tax system was changed to allow married couples to file a joint return in which their combined income would be split in half, with taxes paid on each half regardless of the actual distribution of earnings between the spouses. As a result of this change combined with the progressivity of the tax system, a wife contemplating entry into the labor force would be faced with a tax on her earnings that depended on the level of her husband's earnings. In 1980, for example, a homemaker with two children would face a marginal tax rate of 16 percent on her first dollar earned if her husband earned $10,000 a year, 22 percent if he earned $20,000, and 32 percent if he earned $30,000. Under the system of individual filing that prevailed before 1948, her marginal tax rate was independent of her husband's earnings.

From the point of view of the single person contemplating marriage, the 1948 tax act imposed a "marriage bonus" or "single's penalty" since by marrying someone with little or no income, a person could substantially lower his tax burden. Conversely, the loss of a spouse could entail a rise in tax liability. In 1951, however, a third set of tax rates was enacted for "heads of households" giving, in effect, partial income-splitting privileges to nonmarried persons with dependents.

Meanwhile, single persons without dependents were paying taxes that were as much as 40 percent higher than a married couple with the same amount of taxable income filing a joint return. Responding to the complaints from the growing number of single taxpayers, Congress in 1969 enacted a fourth set of rates for single taxpayers, ensuring that their rates would generally not be higher than 120 percent of the joint return schedule. Married couples choosing to file separately cannot use the new rates for single taxpayers. They must file on a schedule that provides the same rates as the joint schedule but applied to bracket widths that are half as wide. As a result, many two-earner couples pay a combined tax that is considerably higher than the taxes paid by two single persons with the same total income. Taxes of these two-earner couples would fall if they divorced, and taxes of the two employed single persons would rise if they married. It is this feature, dubbed the "marriage penalty," that has recently attracted considerable attention in Congress and in the press. Married two-earner couples were not, however, made worse off as a result of the 1969 act (except indirectly, to the extent that the reduction to single persons resulted in generally higher tax rates than would otherwise be the case). The 1948 legislation which changed the unit of taxation from the individual to the married couple was of much greater significance to the two-earner couples as well as to the married couple in which the wife might have aspired to enter the labor market.

The Tax Unit: Married Couples versus Individuals

Perhaps the subject that generates the most controversy in tax policy is the proper unit of taxation, in particular whether married couples should be taxed based on their combined incomes. The arguments raised involve issues of equity, economic efficiency, and administrative efficiency. I will discuss each of these issues in turn.

Equity Considerations. The traditional equity argument for joint filing is based on the principle of aggregation: married couples with equal combined incomes should pay the same combined taxes regardless of the division of income between the individual partners. The underlying premise is that joint consumption occurs within families who pool their incomes. Thus the individual property rights of family members are of little practical significance. The justification for this point of view is strongly expressed in the report by the Canadian Royal Commission on Taxation (Carter commission, 1966), which advised against the Canadian system of individual filing in the following often quoted passage:

> Taxation of the individual in almost total disregard for his inevitably close financial and economic ties with the other members of the basic social unit of which he is ordinarily a member, the family, is in our view [a] striking instance of the lack of a comprehensive and rational pattern in the present [Canadian] tax system.[5]

The equity argument for joint filing has been challenged on several grounds. One concerns the conflict of joint filing with marriage neutrality, which is another desired principle of a tax system. That is—under a progressive tax system it is impossible to satisfy the aggregation principle and at the same time provide that an individual's tax liability will be unaffected by marriage.[6] As noted, under our current progressive system of joint filing, a worker who marries a nonearner will experience a reduction in taxes; two earners who marry will likely experience a rise in their combined taxes.

The presumption of sharing on which the case for the aggregation principle is based raises some issues in itself. The proportion of husbands and wives who have full and equal command over their combined resources is not known. There are clearly legal limits to the claims of the partner with less wealth or lower earnings. Moreover, a greatly increased probability of divorce may have made husbands and wives more conscious of their individual property rights.[7] The boundaries of sharing units have been confined to married couples, but other units may perform similar functions. Many families contain adults other than husbands and wives. In 1979, for example, 11.3 million children aged twenty years and older were living with their families.[8] Should income splitting be allowed between any related adults living together? Or should the growing group of cohabiting couples who now account for about 3 percent of all couples be included in income splitting?[9] Boundaries for the proper sharing unit are hard to define. They point up, however, the shaky premise underlying the concept of the married couple as a tax unit.

Perhaps the major challenge to the aggregation principle, however, is more pragmatic. It stems from the way we measure income for tax purposes. We have no good way of measuring "full" family income because a substantial portion of it is derived from nonmarket activities. Real income from nonmarket activities varies considerably among couples depending on the amount of time they allocate to such activities. Since one-earner couples systematically have a larger component of unmeasured income than two-earner couples, a policy that seeks to equalize the tax burdens of couples whose pooled money incomes are the same violates the more fundamental principle of ability to pay. Some empirical evidence is now available which permits an assessment of the importance of variation in nonmarket work among families. Because of its significance for tax policy I will digress a bit to summarize the information.

Measuring the volume of nonmarket activities. Since the appearance of Gary Becker's seminal work, "A Theory of the Allocation of Time," in the mid-1960s, economists have been developing conceptual and empirical tools to deal with the measurement of nonmarket time.[10] One recent effort by Martin Murphy and Janice Peskin is particularly pertinent because it provides estimates of the value of household work produced by women with varying amounts of market work.[11] The Murphy-Peskin estimates are based on a survey of hours spent by women and men in different household activities, market work, leisure activities, and sleep. Using estimates of the weighted average market wage rate of workers in similar market occupations, they assigned an hourly value to each of seven types of household work (child care, home repairs, shopping, meal preparation, meal cleanup, cleaning and gardening, and laundry).[12] The Murphy-Peskin estimates do not include the value of leisure time. Only hours of work in activities that produce goods and services that have market equivalents were included.

Basing their findings on time budget data from the Michigan Survey Research Center, Murphy and Martin reported that hours of household work are inversely related to hours of market work. A woman employed full time in the market in 1976 spent twenty hours a week at household work. If she worked part time, she worked thirty-one hours a week in the home. If she was not employed, she spent close to forty-three hours a week doing household work (table 2). The value of household work for the year was estimated to be $4,040 for the woman employed full time, rising to $8,405 for the woman with no market work. The annual earnings from market work for the average full-time employed woman was $8,598 in 1976. Market work, however, entails work-related expenses that home work does not. Estimates by Clair Vickery show that work-related expenses, excluding income taxes, amount to 14 percent of the wife's earnings.[13] Deducting work-related expenses and adding the value of market and home work results in a before-tax "full" income of $11,434 for the woman employed full time, compared with $8,405

6

TABLE 2

Hours Worked and the Value of Work by Women Engaged in Household and Market Activities, 1976

	Average Weekly Hours in Household Work (1)	Average Weekly Hours in Household & Market Work (2)	Annual Value of Household Work (dollars) (3)	Annual Gross Income from Market Work (dollars) (4)	Net Annual[a] Income from Market & Household Work (dollars) (5)
Employment status					
Not employed	42.6	42.6	8,405	—	8,405
Employed part time	31.4	52.2	6,243	3,493	9,247
Employed full time	20.1	66.9	4,040	8,598	11,434

NOTE: Weekly hours are based on a survey of time use of U.S. households in 1975–1976 conducted by the Survey Research Center of the University of Michigan. The valuation of hours is based on "specialist cost," the wage rates of specialists performing similar tasks. Calculations were made by detailed breakdowns of time use within the home.

a. Sum of column (3) and net market income. Net market income is gross market income less a 14 percent deduction for work-related expenses based on estimates by Clair Vickery, "Women's Economic Contribution to the Family," in Ralph E. Smith, ed., *The Subtle Revolution: Women at Work* (Washington, D.C.: The Urban Institute, 1979). Income taxes have not been deducted.

SOURCES: Columns (1), (2), and (3): Murphy and Peskin, "Women at Work in the Home"; column (4): U.S. Bureau of the Census, *Money Income in 1976 of Families and Persons in the United States.*

for the full-time homemaker, a difference of $3,029, not $8,598 as measured by money income alone. Moreover, no account has been taken of the additional twenty-four hours of leisure time a week enjoyed by the full-time homemaker.

If most families derived their incomes from a similar mix of market and home work, the exclusion from the tax base of income from work in the home would pose less of an equity problem. When few married women worked in the market, this was probably the case. The situation now, however, is that the population is divided into sizable groups differing by the proportion of income derived from market and home work. As indicated in table 3, in about one-third of married couples the wife did no market work in 1978. In about 51 percent of the couples,

7

TABLE 3
EARNINGS AND ESTIMATED "FULL" INCOME OF MARRIED COUPLES, BY WORK EXPERIENCE OF HUSBAND AND WIFE, 1978
(dollars)

	Number of Couples (thousands)	Husband's Mean Market Earnings	Wife's Mean Market Earnings	Couple's Mean Combined Market Earnings	Couple's Estimated "Full" Labor Income (mean)[a]
Husband-wife families[b]	47,692	14,126	3,488	17,614	25,539
Husband an earner, wife not an earner	15,787	18,208	—	18,208	27,958
Husband worked year round, full time	12,033	20,827	—	20,827	30,585
Husband and wife earn	24,546	15,735	6,324	22,059	27,496
Husband worked year round, full time	19,122	17,478	6,520	23,998	29,407
Both worked year round, full time	8,954	16,737	9,967	26,704	29,995

a. Estimates include an imputed value for the wife's household work. These values were taken from table 2 according to the employment status of the wife and adjusted for the growth in income between 1976 and 1978. An amount of 14 percent was deducted from the wife's market earnings to account for additional work expenses (but not taxes).

b. Includes couples in which neither work and in which only the wife is an earner.

SOURCE: Population and earnings data: *Money Income of Families and Persons in the United States,* Current Population Reports, P-60, no. 123, pp. 125, 130, 131.

both husbands and wives worked, and of these about one-third consisted of couples in which a husband and a wife worked full time, year round. The remaining 15 percent consisted mainly of retired couples and some couples in which only the wife worked.

Estimates are also given in table 3 of "full" labor income compared with observed money earnings for couples with different proportions of market and home work. The value of untaxed work in the home is imputed for wives according to their work experience categories and based on the estimates of table 2 (adjusted for the change in income between 1976 and 1978). It is clear that pooled money incomes reflect very different amounts of total real income depending on the employment patterns of the wife. In 1978, for example, couples in which both the husband and wife worked full time, year round, received combined market earnings that were 28 percent higher than the earnings of a one-earner family in which the husband worked full time, year round. With progressive taxation, the tax burden of the two-earner couple would have been more than 28 percent higher. Yet on a "full" income basis where the value of work in the home is imputed, the one-earner family would have had the higher income and the higher tax.

These calculations are intended to be illustrative. Different methods for valuing nonmarket time would no doubt give different estimates. It is unlikely, however, that alternative estimates would yield qualitatively different results in terms of implications for tax policy.

Efficient Allocation of Resources. Another major argument against the current system of joint filing for married couples is the effect it has on reducing the incentives of women for market work. In a progressive system the pooling of incomes makes each spouse's marginal tax rate depend on the other's income. The lower-earning spouse, usually the wife, will then be taxed at a higher rate than she would be as an individual. The resulting high marginal tax rates may discourage more than hours of market work. They may also deter investments in human capital as well (though investments in the development of nonmarket skills might be encouraged). As noted in the earlier discussion, as long as nonmarket work and leisure are not taxed, there will be a bias against market work. Income splitting exacerbates the distorting effect of the income tax on the allocation of time between market work and home activities, and this is likely to have a more significant effect on women than on men.

The amount of work shifted out of the market and into household work and leisure will depend on the elasticity of the wife's labor supply function. Because women have been more likely to specialize in home activities than men, their alternatives to market work are broader. Hence, one would expect a more elastic labor supply response of women. A large econometric literature has in fact found almost unanimously that the labor supply of married women is highly sensitive to wage changes, while men's labor supply response is less elastic.[14] Since a tax is essentially a reduction in the wage, it is expected that married women would be sensitive to changes in tax rates. This has been found to be the case in studies that explicitly take taxes into account.[15]

As noted, income splitting produces a situation in which the marginal tax rate faced by working husbands and wives depends on their

9

TABLE 4

LABOR FORCE PARTICIPATION RATES OF MARRIED WOMEN WITH
CHILDREN UNDER EIGHTEEN IN 1978, BY YEARS OF SCHOOLING
COMPLETED AND INCOME OF HUSBAND IN 1977
(percent)

Income of Husband (dollars)		Years of Schooling Completed by Wife		
	Total[a]	0 to 11 years	12 years	16 years
5,000– 6,999	50.6	42.9	56.1	[b]
7,000– 9,999	54.9	48.6	56.8	75.6
10,000–12,999	56.7	49.4	56.4	68.5
13,000–14,999	54.6	44.3	54.9	58.2
15,000–19,999	51.3	39.8	51.7	55.2
20,000–24,999	46.1	36.4	44.6	49.5
25,000–34,999	40.3	33.3	34.4	48.5
35,000–49,999	38.0	[b]	35.8	46.8
50,000 and over	26.7	[b]	23.7	24.6

NOTE: Labor force participation rates are given as a percentage of population.
a. Total includes wives with amounts of schooling other than shown separately.
b. Base is less than 75,000 persons.
SOURCE: Bureau of Labor Statistics, U.S. Department of Labor, "Marital and Family Characteristics of Workers, 1970 to 1978," Special Labor Force Report 219, table H.

averaged incomes.[16] Since a wife usually earns less than her husband, the wife's marginal tax is raised (and the husband's lowered) compared with what it would be in a tax system with individual filing. Because of the greater sensitivity of working wives' labor supply to tax rates, the increase in hours worked by wives as a result of reducing their tax rates would exceed any reduction in hours worked by husbands as a result of a rise in their marginal rates. The largest response in labor supply would come from women married to high-income men. As indicated in table 4, the labor force participation rate of married women —holding constant their education and the presence of children— declines as husbands' incomes rise, particularly after husbands' incomes reach $20,000 a year. This in part demonstrates an "income effect." (Since the table adjusts for the wife's education, her potential before-tax wage is roughly held constant.) It is also likely, however, to reflect the effect of the rising marginal tax rate associated with husbands' rising incomes. A reduction in the marginal tax rate facing married women is likely to induce an increase in labor force participation of

married persons were felt to bear a particular burden when required to provide both financial and child-care support. A similar situation, however, prevails for two-earner couples with children. Moreover, the dependent need not be a child for the taxpayer to qualify for head-of-household status.

Summary and Policy Alternatives

The issue of defining the taxpaying unit becomes highly significant in a progressive tax system. The issue is further heightened by the fact that taxable income is restricted to income produced in the market. The current U.S. tax system treats a married couple as one tax unit. Thus the tax liability of married couples is based on their combined money incomes only. Both efficiency problems and equity problems are raised.

An efficiency issue arises under the joint filing rule because a married woman, who by tradition has the wider choice between market and nonmarket uses of her time, is taxed on her first dollar earned at the rate applicable to the last dollar earned by her husband. A wife's marginal tax rate is, therefore, tied to her husband's income. The higher his income, the higher her marginal tax rate. Empirical evidence strongly shows that the labor supply of married women is more responsive to changes in marginal tax rates than is the labor supply of married men. Thus, a system of joint filing is likely to discourage the market employment of married women. In addition, any tax that is restricted to market earnings has an inherent bias against market work, since work in the home is not taxed. A progressive tax with joint filing exaggerates the bias.

Joint filing has also been criticized on equity grounds. The major argument stems from the exclusion of income from nonmarket activities from the tax base. When the money income of each spouse is combined, the two-earner couple is pushed into a higher tax bracket than a one-earner couple with equivalent "full income." (Full income is a measure of income that includes the value of work in the home and deducts additional work expenses associated with market work.) The principle that couples with the same money income should pay the same tax regardless of the division of income between them is of questionable merit if the major reason that the wife's share differs is the extent to which she works in the market.

Another complex issue involves the question of sharing in a marriage. Does each spouse truly share the income and wealth of the other? Do we know enough about the answer to this question to base tax policy on it? A third equity issue concerns the marriage neutrality of the system. If a progressive tax system adopts income splitting, an individual's tax status changes with marriage. Because of the additional complication of different schedules for single taxpayers and taxpayers who are unmarried heads of households, the system produces an array of marriage penalties and marriage bonuses depending on marital and earnings status. Thus, marriage incentives as well as earnings incentives may be distorted by the tax.

Several policy alternatives have been proposed to remedy these equity and efficiency issues. A recent change in the tax law has also taken a significant step toward modifying the situation. The Tax Act of 1981 affects the tax liability of married couples by providing a tax deduction on the earnings of the lower-earning spouse of 5 percent of earnings in 1982 and 10 percent in 1983, up to earnings of $30,000 (a maximum deduction of $3,000 in 1983). The new law will reduce the marginal tax rates of most married women (that is, for those earning less than the cap), but probably will not reduce them to the level these women would pay if single. Moreover, a wife's marginal tax rate would still be tied to her husband's income. The marriage penalty will be reduced but not eliminated, and the effect will vary among couples depending on their level of income and the division of income between spouses.[22]

An individual filing system raising the same total revenues as current law would likely reduce the marginal tax rates of most married women considerably more than provided by the new deduction for the second earner. All individuals, regardless of marital status, would face the same schedule of tax rates and could evaluate market work choices under the same set of tax rules. Individual filing would then fully eliminate the marriage bonus and the marriage penalty. Administrative difficulties could arise with respect to the treatment of property income, but they do not seem to be an insurmountable obstacle, as the experience of other countries with individual filing would seem to indicate.

Another alternative that would eliminate the problem of the proper tax unit is the adoption of a single proportional rate schedule for all categories of taxpayers. All taxpayers would face the same marginal rates, the tax system would be marriage neutral, and couples with equal money incomes would pay equivalent taxes regardless of the division of income between them. Eliminating the progressivity of the income tax system, of course, is an issue involving wider considerations than the tax treatment of the family, and these considerations must be evaluated. A less radical schedule, however, could be constructed which would still allow some progressivity and at the same time equalize marginal tax rates and provide marriage neutrality for most taxpayers.

In sum, the change in the new tax law regarding the tax treatment of the family will improve incentives for market work among married women. The marginal tax rates applicable to individuals with the same potential earnings will still differ, however, because of marital status and because of a spouse's income. Nor will the marriage penalty be eliminated. Two alternatives—individual filing and the flattening out of the tax schedule—would correct these problems and move the system much closer to an optimum. They would not provide neutrality between income from market and nonmarket uses of time, something that cannot occur until we learn how to measure the imputed income from nonmarket activities. They would, however, reduce the current additional bias imposed by the tax structure. Simulations are needed to estimate labor supply consequences, distributional consequences, and the revenue effects of possible alternatives.[23] It would also be helpful to impute income from home work for evaluating distributional consequences.

Family Issues in Social Security

Many of the same problems that have arisen regarding the treatment of the family in the income tax system have been applied to the social security system. The social security system through its tax and benefit structure provides subsidies to married couples in which one spouse has little or no covered employment. This situation clearly benefits the "traditional" family in which the wife is a dependent—and raises many of the same equity and efficiency questions that apply to the income tax system. It has also attracted strong criticism from single workers and two-earner couples who perceive that they are being excluded from a free ride for which they pay in the form of higher taxes.

Under current law, generally speaking, the wife of a covered worker may receive retirement benefits equal to the higher of the social security benefit based on her own earnings record or 50 percent of her husband's benefit. Upon the death of her husband, a widow may receive a benefit equal to 100 percent of her husband's benefit or her own benefit, whichever is higher.[24] If a wife works in covered employment, she will only benefit from the spouse's provision if her own earned benefit is less than her entitlement as a dependent spouse or widow. Since social security taxes are levied on individuals, not families, the married woman will pay social security taxes on the same basis as everyone else, including men whose wives are homemakers.

Social security tax payments made into the system over the work life are tied to benefits received at retirement. It is reasonable, therefore, to look at the payoff to social security taxes as a way of evaluating the system. Several years ago I estimated rates of return to social security tax payments for the cohort entering covered employment in 1976.[25] Estimates were made for married couples according to the number of

15

years of work experience of the wife. As expected, the rate of return (in real terms) falls as wives' work experience increases, dropping from 2.2 percent in the case of wives having no covered employment to 1 percent in the case of wives having the maximum work experience (thirty-nine years of covered employment). As the wife increases her work experience, and hence her earnings, an increasing amount of the spouse benefit is forfeited. Thus, more is added to the couple's tax payments than to its social security benefits as the wife's years of employment rise.

The rate-of-return calculations illustrate the equity issue arising from the spouse's benefit. It is also difficult to justify the transfer on welfare grounds, since it is based on homemaker status rather than evidence of need. The benefit amount is tied to the husband's earnings, and as shown previously, women who are homemakers tend to be married to men with higher earnings. The redistributive implications are hardly persuasive.

In terms of economic efficiency, the dependent's benefit introduces still another disincentive to paid employment. By providing an extra benefit for unpaid work in the home, it adds to the bias against market work which is ingrained in the tax system.

One alternative to the current system would be to phase out spouse's benefits gradually. Such a change would move social security in the direction of a straightforward compulsory pension system. Only workers would pay taxes, and only workers would collect benefits.

Issues would be raised, however, about the coverage of married women who typically still withdraw from the labor force for some number of years and are, therefore, less likely to obtain work-related pensions. Moreover, most will likely outlive their husbands by quite a few years, and provision by husbands for their surviving spouses may not be reliable. The drawbacks of dependents' benefits have been noted. If social security is viewed as mandatory saving for a basic retirement benefit, then one can argue that the requirement be extended to those who choose nonmarket over market work. The challenge is to design a plan that will enable women who choose to be homemakers for significant periods of time to acquire a retirement benefit that they can count on, regardless of divorce or death of spouse. At the same time the benefit should not impose a burden on two-earner couples and other taxpayers. Various plans have been suggested, and they differ in the extent to which they are focused on the family rather than the individual.

One popular proposal calls for "earnings sharing"—dividing the total covered earnings of a couple in half each year to create two independent earnings records. In the more comprehensive plans, these earnings records would be the basis for all retirement, disability, and (with an inheritance provision) survivors' benefits, totally replacing dependent's benefits. Supporters stress that an earnings sharing arrangement formally acknowledges the economic contribution of the homemaker and treats marriage as a partnership in which men and women are equal. Although many would view this feature as a strong point of the plan, others may view it as a disadvantage. In the event of a divorce, the spouse with lower earnings would gain from earnings sharing, but at the expense of the spouse with higher earnings, whose future benefits would be lowered. All husbands and wives may not, in fact, contribute half the family's total income (including the value of work in the home), and an argument can be made that the relative contributions of spouses should best be left to families and divorce courts to determine. Many of the same issues raised by the income tax provision for income splitting are also raised by earnings sharing. The social security benefit structure is progressive. Thus, a married worker who does not get divorced and who splits his earnings with a homemaker spouse will receive a higher benefit on the two halves combined than a worker with equivalent earnings who is single or who is married to a spouse with earnings. The implicit rate of return to social security tax payments would still differ by marital status and by earnings status of spouse, but not as much as under the current system. Moving to a proportional benefit formula would, however, be one response to this problem.

Another proposal would treat the homemaker as an individual worker. It is not feasible to impute a value to work in the home for individual homemakers. Work at home, however, could be credited at an arbitrary amount, and taxes could be paid on that amount as though the homemaker were a self-employed worker.[26] In this way, all women would acquire their own earnings record without gaps for time taken to care for children and provide other homemaking services. The credits would replace demeaning dependents' benefits. Disincentives to paid work would be greatly reduced, since unpaid work at home would be at least partially subject to taxation. Single individuals and two-earner couples would no longer be subsidizing one-earner couples.

Home-time credits could be mandatory or optional. The objection to optional payments is that those for whom the rationale for social security is greatest—that is, those who lack the self-discipline to save for their old age—might opt out of a voluntary plan. An optional feature could, however, be added to a basic mandatory credit, permitting additional credits to be accumulated through higher contributions. The progressivity of the social security benefit formula raises an issue here as it does with earnings sharing. Homemakers would receive the benefit of the tilt in the formula if they paid taxes on the schedule of a low-wage worker, which may or may not be a desirable feature. Presumably all features of the benefit structure would be reexamined if a change in dependents' benefits were considered, and progressivity would be an important issue.

Because implementing self-financed home-time credits or earnings sharing would be a radical change from the current system, it would be necessary to phase them in over a period of time. Self-financed credits would, however, provide an increase in tax revenues that would exceed new benefit payments and would in this respect improve the financing of the system.

Conclusions

Taken together, the social security system and the income tax system reflect very similar attitudes about the role of women in the family and in society. The fact that income from homemaking activities is exempt from taxation imposes a fundamental bias toward work in the home. Both systems, however, provide additional pecuniary incentives for the formation of husband-wife families in which the wife is a full-time home-maker.

The income tax, through joint filing and the provision for income splitting, imposes a high marginal tax rate on the married woman and thereby reduces her return to paid employment. This outcome is the result of the interaction of a progressive tax system with adherence to the principle that the married couple should be treated as a single tax unit so that all married couples with the same money income would pay the same tax. The underlying philosophy is that married couples share their income so completely that individual taxation would be illogical. Three challenges to the argument have been given. One is that money income is a highly misleading indication of ability to pay when couples vary significantly, as they do, in the extent to which the wife produces nontaxed goods and services in the home. If the goal is to tax couples with equal "full income" equally, it may well be better met by individual taxation than by joint taxation. A second issue concerns the assumption of full sharing in a marriage. Unless property and income are legally transferred, each spouse may not in fact have full and equal command over the couple's total resources. A third argument is that the tax system cannot be marriage neutral under joint filing and progressivity. Moreover, this is exacerbated by maintaining a separate tax schedule for single taxpayers.

Unlike the income tax, the social security system levies a tax on an individual basis, but bases benefits on the family unit. By providing dependents' benefits for spouses of retired workers and for widows, social security provides outright subsidies to full-time homemakers. The more a married woman works for pay in the market, the lower will be her return from social security tax payments—that is, beyond what she would have received as a dependent spouse.

The effect of both the income tax and social security is to encourage women to devote themselves to family responsibilities. Those who see women's primary role as homemaker would likely prefer the status quo. Those who place a high value on a system that minimizes disincentives for market work are more likely to favor a change to a system of individual filing in the income tax or a system of proportional (or close to proportional) tax rates. This would be consistent with a social security system that provides benefits for covered workers only, thus eliminating dependents' benefits, or with a system in which pensions for homemakers are self-financed through home-time credits. Although earnings sharing in social security is often proposed as a way of ameliorating the problem of the two-earner couple, it is philosophically more akin to joint filing in the income tax. Marital earnings are assumed to be equally and jointly produced, and benefits to couples with the same money earnings would be equalized. Although earnings sharing would reduce the more extreme work disincentive of the dependent's benefit, it would still provide a greater implicit rate of return to the homemaker than to the wife with market earnings or to the single person.

The essential features of the income tax and social security programs were put into place several decades ago when the options women faced were quite different from those of today. Market forces and social changes have provided powerful incentives for women to shift into market work, and they have done so. Without the disincentives of the tax and social security systems, it is likely that the transition would have been more rapid. Whether the social consequences of a more rapid transition would have been beneficial or traumatic is unknown.

I would like to end with a comment that Boris Bittker made in the concluding remarks of his comprehensive essay on the taxation of the family:

> Theoreticians, whatever their backgrounds, cannot "solve" the problem of taxing family income. They can identify the issues that must be resolved, point out conflicts among the objectives to be served, propose alternative approaches, and predict the outcome of picking one route rather than another. Having performed these functions, the expert must give way to the citizen, whose judgments in the end can rest on nothing more precise or permanent than collective social preferences. Once the citizenry casts the die, however, the expert is entitled to offer a postscript, namely, that the chosen solution will itself turn out, sooner or later, to be a problem.[27]

Notes

1. As expressed in the Revenue Act of 1916, ch. 463, 39 stat. 756.

2. Alicia H. Munnell, "The Couple versus the Individual under the Federal Personal Income Tax," in Henry J. Aaron and Michael J. Boskin, eds., *The Economics of Taxation* (Washington, D.C.: Brookings Institution, 1980).

3. Lucas v. Earl, 281 U.S. 111(1930); the Supreme Court also ruled in 1930 in Poe v. Sanborn, 282 U.S. 101(1930), and in three companion cases that one-half of the community income of a couple was taxable to each spouse. The history of legislation and other events surrounding the change in the tax unit is discussed in more detail in Boris I. Bittker, "Federal Income Taxation and the Family," *Stanford Law Review*, vol. 27, no. 6 (1975), pp. 1391–1463.

4. Although in Poe v. Sanborn it was held that community property laws were applicable for federal tax purposes, Fernandez v. Wiener, 325 U.S. 340(1945), is usually cited to indicate that a definition of property can supersede the state definition for tax purposes. (See Committee on Ways and Means, Hearing before the House of Representatives on the Tax Treatment of Married, Head of Household, and Single Taxpayers, April 2 and 3, 1980, Serial 96–93).

5. Royal Commission on Taxation, *Report of the Royal Commission on Taxation*, vol. 3 (Ottawa, 1966).

6. The impossibility of simultaneously satisfying the three principles has been formally demonstrated by several tax theorists (Bittker, "Federal Income Taxation and the Family").

7. The divorce rate (per married woman) doubled between 1965 and 1979. Based on an analysis of the June 1975 Current Population Survey, estimates made by Thomas Espenshade at the Urban Institute show that the probability a marriage would end in divorce was 30 percent for females in the mid-1970s.

8. U.S. Bureau of the Census, *Marital Status and Living Arrangements: March 1979*, Current Population Report, Series P-20, no. 349, 1980.

9. Ibid. In 1979, 1.3 million cohabiting couples were reported by the Current Population Survey, up from 523,000 in 1970.

10. Gary S. Becker, "A Theory of the Allocation of Time," *Economic Journal*, vol. 75 (1965), pp. 493–517. See also Reuben Gronau, "The Intrafamily Allocation of the Housewives' Time," *American Economic Review*, vol. 63, no. 4 (1973), pp. 534–651; idem, "Home Production: A Forgotten Industry," mimeographed, National Bureau of Economic Research and Hebrew University, August 1977; James Heckman, "Shadow Prices, Market Wages, and Labor Supply," *Econometrica*, vol. 42 (1974), pp. 679–94; Frank Stafford and Greg Duncan, "The Use of Time and Technology by Households in the United States," *Research in Labor Economics*, vol. 3 (Greenwich, Conn.: JAI Press Inc., 1980); Ismail A. Sirageldin, *Non-Market*

Components of National Income (Ann Arbor: Survey Research Center, Institute for Social Research, The University of Michigan, 1969).

11. Martin Murphy and Janice Peskin, "Women at Work in the Home," Paper presented at the American Statistical Association Meetings, Detroit, Michigan, August 1981.

12. This "specialist cost" technique of valuing hours essentially provides the labor cost valued by the market wage of specialists who perform similar activities in the market. It will be biased upward or downward if homemakers are less (or more) skilled than market specialists. Since labor costs are only a component of the market price of service goods, the use of wage rates would bias the estimates downward. Another downward bias results from the fact that the time use data only report the primary activity, and it is often the case that a household worker produces two kinds of output at once—for example, laundry and child care. Unless the homemaker is much less efficient than market workers, the net bias is likely to be downward. Other techniques for valuing time have been used in several studies, and Martin and Murphy provide some alternative estimates using different techniques. The valuation of time by the opportunity wage method (see Gronau, "Intrafamily Allocation," and Heckman, "Shadow Prices") yields higher estimates that vary among individuals depending on their possible market wage. Specialist cost measures vary only by the mix of activities.

13. Clair Vickery, "Women's Economic Contribution to the Family," in Ralph E. Smith, ed., *The Subtle Revolution: Women at Work* (Washington, D.C.: The Urban Institute, 1979).

14. See Orley Ashenfelter and James Heckman, "The Estimation of Income and Substitution Effects in a Model of Family Labor Supply," *Econometrica*, vol. 42 (1974), pp. 73–85; M. J. Boskin, "The Economics of Labor Supply," in G. Cain and H. Watts, eds., *Income Maintenance and Labour Supply* (New York: Rand McNally, 1973); Heckman, "Shadow Prices"; Marvin Kosters, "Effects of an Income Tax on Labor Supply," in Arnold C. Harberger and Martin J. Bailey, eds., *The Taxation of Income from Capital* (Washington, D.C.: Brookings Institution, 1969); Jacob Mincer, "Labor Force Participation of Married Women," in G. Lewis, ed., *Aspects of Labor Economics,* Universities–National Bureau Conference Series, no. 14 (Princeton, N.J., 1962).

15. Harvey S. Rosen, "Applications of Optimal Tax Theory to Problems in Taxing Families and Individuals," Office of Tax Analysis Paper 21, November 1976.

16. For the wife who is contemplating working, the marginal tax rate is based on her husband's income.

17. Rosen, "Applications of Optimal Tax Theory."

18. These calculations are based on the 1980 tax schedules. The 1983 rates will all be scaled down as a result of the across-the-board tax cuts. Because of the greater sensitivity of women's hours of work to tax changes, one would expect a positive effect of the tax cut on women's labor force participation.

19. Munnell, "The Couple versus the Individual."

20. See the discussion in Joseph A. Pechman, *Federal Tax Policy*, 3rd ed., (Washington, D.C.: Brookings Institution, 1977), of the relationship of the exemptions to the poverty line.

21. Douglas Wolf, *Income Maintenance and the Dynamics of Household Composition*, Paper presented at the Annual Meeting of the Society for the Study of Social Problems, 1976.

22. Couples with higher incomes and a more equal division of income between the spouses will receive the least relief though they now pay the largest marriage penalty. Others (two-earner couples with a very unequal division of income between them) will receive a larger marriage bonus than before. See the estimates of similar proposals in "The Income Tax Treatment of Married Couples and Single Persons," A Report of the Joint Committee on Taxation, Washington, D.C., April, 2, 1980.

23. The study in this volume by Daniel Feenberg provides such estimates for the Tax Act of 1981 compared with earlier law.

24. Spouse's and surviving spouse's benefits are available to both women and men, although in practice women are more likely to qualify than men. The exact amount of dependent's benefit received depends on the age of the spouse at retirement and other factors.

25. These estimates were based on projections of lifetime earnings profiles and assumptions about real growth and mortality. Actual wage histories of women with varying numbers of years of covered earnings were used to project women's future earnings streams. Longitudinal age-earnings profiles for men were projected from cross-sectional observations on earnings by age. The calculations assume a Hsiao-type price-indexed system that is balanced. See June O'Neill, *Returns to Social Security*, Paper presented at the American Economic Association meetings, September 1976.

26. Without the feature of self-financing, a system of homemaker credits is simply dependents' benefits with a name change.

27. Bittker, "Federal Income Taxation and the Family."

Commentary

Joseph J. Minarik

June O'Neill's paper discusses both the income tax and social security. In the first case the author argues for mandatory separate filing for married persons, and in the second she argues against the spouse's benefit as presently constituted. I shall discuss first the equity and then the efficiency arguments that O'Neill raises for mandatory separate filing, and then policy alternatives to mandatory separate filing. Finally, I shall briefly consider the spouse's benefit under social security.

On the basis of equity, the author favors individual filing because:

1. Contrary to the present system, in which we assume equal sharing of income in marriages, we do not really know the extent to which income is shared between spouses.

2. The probability of divorce is increasing, and therefore the degree of sharing of income between spouses might very well be reduced from what it once was.

3. There is a great deal of income from nonmarket activities not recognized under the present tax system, and if we were to tax that income, taxes for single-earner married couples would be higher.

4. There are now many diverse family arrangements, including cohabitation and the presence of older children who can provide nonmarket income to the family; if we cannot cope with those arrangements, we might as well ignore marriage as the tax unit and go back to individual filing.

I disagree with all these arguments for mandatory single filing because of one general premise: the basic decision-making, consuming, and saving unit is the family. An individual's potential for consumption and saving is greater, the greater the income of his or her spouse. Given this fundamental interdependence between the abilities of spouses to pay, mandatory separate filing must misestimate couples' ability to pay. In my judgment, O'Neill's specific arguments do not override this general premise.

On the first point, if the degree of income sharing in marriages is uncertain, should we leap to the conclusion that the degree of sharing is zero and go immediately to mandatory separate filing? If, as in many marriages today, one spouse works outside the home and the other spouse does not, and the spouse who does not earn manages to fend off exposure and starvation, that is an indication that there is some sharing going on. Mandatory separate filing would eliminate the tax system's recognition of this obvious sharing. Even in two-earner marriages there is, generally, some degree of income sharing that ought to be recognized in the tax code. Enjoyment of some of the most fundamental and important family expenditures, such as the purchase of housing services and the food on the table, is clearly joint. The protection of the couple's savings is generally shared. This interdependence of the economic statuses of the spouses strongly supports joint filing, even in marriages where financial affairs are nominally kept separate.

Regarding O'Neill's second argument, if 30 percent of all marriages end in divorce, should all marriages have zero tax consequences? Here again the answer is no. Beyond the sharing consequences of extant marriages discussed earlier, even divorce settlements require sharing in their provision of alimony and child support. Therefore, in many cases the decision to marry is a commitment to sharing even beyond the duration of the marriage. Even without these arguments, however, patterning the tax code after the 30 percent of marriages that end in divorce seems akin to leaving your umbrella at home because the probability of rain is only 70 percent.

Regarding the third argument, if we cannot tax the imputed income from work in the home by nonearning spouses (or others), should we switch to mandatory separate filing? This is surely the most complex argument. In the abstract, a tax on home labor would have pros and cons. George Bernard Shaw aside, home labor does produce income, and we do profess (in our less guarded moments) to tax all income. Complications arise in that the tax on home labor would have to be paid in unrealized cash, meaning that the family's mix of cash and noncash income (which should be irrelevant) would make the tax more or less burdensome. Further, individual productivities in home labor are immeasurable, meaning the amount of home-produced income to be taxed would be uncertain.

O'Neill suggests that mandatory separate filing would be superior in light of the nontaxation of home income. The correspondence of mandatory separate filing to taxation of home-produced income is extremely tenuous, however, if not nonexistent. If we simply consider one-earner couples exclusively, mandatory separate filing in the otherwise unchanged present system and in the absence of any evaluation of the actual home production of the nonworking spouse would amount to a tax on his or her time. The amount of the tax would be a function not of the services received, but of the family's other income. No further changes in the tax law, apart from an actual valuation of home production, would take account of the variation in home-produced income. This home production rationale for separate filing is even more bizarre when one considers that it would affect the taxes of two-earner couples, where home production is not in question. The rationale would also questionably justify selective tax increases for one-earner families in which the second spouse cannot find market work because it is not available, the second spouse cannot accept market work because child care of sufficient quality is not available, or both spouses believe that children should be raised in the home by one of their natural parents. In these cases and where the working spouse has a modest income, mandatory separate filing would cause hardship.

In regard to O'Neill's fourth argument, if we cannot determine tax policies for cohabitation or for twenty-year-old and older children in the home, should we give up on determining a coherent tax policy for the institution of marriage entirely? Again the answer is no. We may not be able to deal with some of the most complicated household formulations, but for the purposes of taxation we ought to be dealing with the basic institution of marriage to the extent that it exists.

In summary, if we do have competing principles of aggregation—on the one hand, the principle that households with equal income should pay equal taxes regardless of how much each individual earns and, on the other hand, the principle of marriage neutrality whereby we attempt to maintain equal taxation of individuals whether they marry or not—then we may want to compromise in the direction of marriage neutrality, as in the current law's deduction for the lesser-earning spouse, but we should not throw the aggregation principle entirely out the window.

O'Neill also argues for individual filing on grounds of efficiency. She contends that since the wife's marginal tax rate depends upon the husband's income, this imposes an efficiency cost and discourages women from work. As empirical verification, she cites the falling labor force participation of wives as husbands' incomes increase and claims that this demonstrates the potential for greater female labor supply.

Although this effect is probably positive as O'Neill argues, the magnitude is probably not very different from zero. The drop in wives' labor force participation as husbands' incomes increase is the product of not only a price (tax rate) effect but also an income effect. Further, the recent and concurrent increases of female labor force participation and the speed of marginal tax rate bracket creep (based on husbands' as well as total incomes) suggest that the link between participation and taxes is somewhat tenuous. We might also ask just how much more rapid the increase in female labor supply could possibly be.

Beyond these pure efficiency arguments, the equity and efficiency issues are interrelated. It is very reasonable, for example, that there be some reduction of the marginal tax rate of a married woman who decides to leave home and go to work as a photographer for *Ladies Home Journal*. The current law provides this. If the husband of that woman, however, happens to be a Greek shipping magnate and the richest man in the world, there is questionable merit to starting her all the way down at the bottom of the tax rate schedule. If we believe that the abilities to pay of the spouses are interdependent, then it is inevitable that there be some dependence of the marginal tax rate of one spouse upon the earnings of the other if equity principles are to be maintained.

The administrative problems of a switch to separate filing should not be underestimated. The "dependent shopping" problem that O'Neill identifies with the present system would be no easier. The problems of allocation of deductions and property income between spouses would be considerable. Finally, there would be more and more complicated pieces of paper to fill out and review.

In summary, there are two legitimate issues to be addressed: (1) lower marginal tax rates for working spouses would be desirable and (2) marriage penalties are so high in some cases as to induce behavior that depreciates both the institution of marriage and the federal tax system. Mandatory separate filing addresses these two issues, though (it is argued here) at excessive costs in terms of equity. Optional separate filing would also address these issues, though it would beg the equity question and its revenue cost would be considerable. The deduction for second earners in the Economic Recovery Tax Act ameliorates both problems, but its effect on marginal tax rates is more limited and some large marriage penalties remain. Although a costless solution to these two problems does not exist, there are ways to ameliorate both of them. The amount of the marriage penalty is a function of the parameters of the tax law, and alternative combinations of low-income relief and marginal tax rate brackets could be designed to reduce the penalty, with minimal disturbance to the overall distribution of tax liabilities. If future tax changes (including those scheduled under the Economic Recovery Tax Act) were made with the marriage penalty in mind, this problem could be eased. And, of course, the overall level of marginal tax rates is a function of the size of the tax base and the desired yield. These factors are subject to policy intervention.

One might also quarrel with O'Neill's assessment of the social security system in general, and the spouse's benefit in particular. The spouse's benefit provides protection in old age to those whose lower earning records to retirement indicate a likelihood of difficulty in support-ing themselves. It is less questionable on welfare grounds than O'Neill paints it to be. Although it is true that nonworking spouses of high earners piggyback on those high earning records, it is also true that nonworking spouses of low earners benefit from the progressive (that is, pro–low earners) benefit formula. Simply phasing out the spouse's benefit, one of O'Neill's options, would eliminate this important protec-tive function which is uniquely the role of social insurance. We may wish to have earners with nonworking spouses bear the cost of the spouse's benefit through some form of payroll tax surcharge, though the added burden on lower-income families would have to be considered. The problem of divorced homemakers could be addressed here, though this would increase the scope of the system and the size of the total tax burden.

In general review, I do not find the income tax and social security systems to be "demeaning" or to provide "incentives for the formation of husband-wife families in which the wife is a full-time homemaker," as O'Neill does. Neither the tax law nor the social security law makes reference to sex (except in the social security system's lower retirement ages for women, which are only tangentially relevant here). The issues of the marriage penalty and marginal tax rates are relevant to both men and women.

In our zeal to provide the most sex- and behavior-neutral tax and benefit systems, we must not lose sight of basic equity principles. In a revenue-constrained world, large tax cuts for high-income two-earner couples, such as mandatory separate filing would provide, have to be made up by someone else. If we look hard enough, we can find struc-tural changes that provide significant efficiency gains without moving the tax burden farther down the income scale.

Edwin Cohen

I am accustomed to speaking on short notice on the subject of taxation of the family or, rather, the comparative taxation of married and single persons. That is probably the only way I have ever talked about the subject. The first time was in the spring of 1972 when Wilbur Mills was the chairman of the House Ways and Means Committee. I think that he decided that he did not want any discussion of general tax revision in 1972, so in one week he scheduled three hearings on three very difficult and different subjects, the first of which was the taxation of married and single persons. Gerry Brannon and I—and possibly Emil Sunley—put together testimony on this subject.

I testified just ahead of Gloria Swanson and Vivian Kellems, who were most articulate witnesses and very determined to demonstrate that they, as single persons, were being discriminated against. After them came witnesses who were married persons who were equally determined to prove that the system discriminated against them.

I remember very well working particularly with Gerry, and possibly with Emil also, and coming to the conclusion—a conclusion that was then new to me but mathematically demonstrable—that if you have a system of graduated income tax rates and if you believe as the Congress determined in 1948 that married couples that had some aggregate taxable incomes should pay the same tax, the problem was mathematically insoluble. There is no solution that will clearly and fairly balance the tax burden on married and single persons.

Then we come to the point that I think June O'Neill has come to—do we choose to have a system of income taxation in which each individual is subject to tax on his or her own taxable income regardless of the marriage status and regardless of the income or deductions of other members of the family unit? (I personally come to the other conclusion, and I do so in part I guess because as a practicing lawyer, even though I am a sometime professor and am old enough to have practiced under the system before 1948, I think a system of individual taxation, at least in this country, would as a practical matter be impossible to operate or at least quite inadvisable to operate.)

It is hard to go back—what is it, thirty-three years—to the time before 1948 in the common law states. The community property states had solved the problem for themselves under *Poe* v. *Seaborn* in the Supreme Court. In the common law states, however, we had the problems of family partnerships in which husbands and wives tried to shift income among themselves by means of various forms of partnerships, followed inevitably by much litigation, followed by a family partnership rule that works to a fairly good extent with respect to children as partners, but that I feel would not work with respect to husbands and wives.

Then, with respect to property income, you have transfers in trust, most of which have been eliminated because there is no particular advantage for moving income between husband and wife by trust. You have the problems of gifts, putting income in one or another person's name by registering securities in their names and determining whether there is really a transfer of title or only a nominee situation. You have husbands paying salaries to wives in the family enterprise and vice versa. You have problems as to who takes deductions. For example, did the wife make a charitable deduction out of household money or out of her own money? Who is entitled to the deduction for the real estate tax on the family home, or for interest on the mortgage on the home?

We find that the Congress, through the Internal Revenue Code, repeatedly tries to eliminate this problem. I illustrate this with respect to, say, the old $100 dividends-received deduction which was limited to each spouse, making it necessary to list on the tax return whether the dividend income was that of the husband or the wife because the $100 was calculated separately. To simplify matters, the Congress has now combined the deduction, so it is immaterial which spouse has the dividend income.

The marital deduction in the estate and gift tax is an effort to see that property at death can pass without tax from one spouse to the other because of marital status. It greatly simplifies the planning of estates. Throughout the code, you have to treat husband and wife together for many purposes—determining personal holding companies, disallowing losses on transfers between spouses, and so on. In the whole gambit of those rules, I would find it extremely difficult to revert to a system in which each spouse reported his or her net taxable income separately.

Beyond that—and this is not based upon my experience as a lawyer but upon my particular view of the marital relationship—it seems to me that in a well-functioning marriage, it is immaterial whose income it is and who pays the expenses. They are shared by household payments from one person to another, and I think that is the ideal marriage. To try to break that down so that husband and wife decide who gets the income in order to make them roughly equal is contrary to the way the whole system has been going for a long time. So I would come to the conclusion that I would not choose individual income taxation of spouses.

With respect to studies about nonmarket income for the nonworking spouse who spends her hours at home, I have complete sympathy for the problem of the spouse who performs the household chores, a thankless task. I am a very well-trained butler, and I clean up very well. I am a well-trained and experienced baby sitter. Of course, my rates are high because I consider it the most difficult type of work that one can do.

Now I can imagine a system in which we treat nonmarket income and leisure time as taxable income. I got up at six this morning and played tennis for an hour. Whether I should be taxed for that privilege or rewarded for it, I do not know, but if we go to a system of that kind, I am perfectly willing to take into account for income tax purposes the nonmarket income of a spouse, but not otherwise. My secretary, who happens not to be married, has many of these chores to perform for herself while she maintains her own household, and my wife and I each have problems of this kind, but I find it impossible to measure those amounts in an income tax system. If we are not going to measure them for each and every person, I see no basis for measuring them solely in the case of the married couple, where the spouse is working part time or full time, because everyone has those cares and duties to perform regardless of marital status.

I might say that I find the whole subject difficult, of course, but I believe that you have to be practical. You cannot solve all the problems of taxation to make everything equal. Life just does not produce complete equality.

I guess the most pointed letter I ever received while I was at the Treasury came from an unmarried lady in Ohio when we were about to reduce the tax burden on single persons. Like so many others, she wrote complaining about the burden on single persons, and when I got to the bottom of the letter, it was signed, "Sincerely, Mary." I had never known the lady before, and I noticed there was an asterisk after the signature "Mary" and a footnote that read, "I hope you will pardon the familiarity, but I've been sending you so much money over such a long period of time that I thought we ought to be on a first-name basis."

Obviously people feel very strongly about this matter, but I think that you cannot solve it to everyone's satisfaction. I think it is an insoluble problem. You can move it around a bit to shift the relative burdens, but there is no easy or complete solution.

I might say in closing that I think there are several subdivisions of the problem that we might discuss, but I will not try to discuss each of them at the moment. One is the rate structure, but a second is the personal exemption, and a third is what we used to call the minimum standard deduction, later the low-income allowance, now the zero-bracket amount. This third allowance was designed when my group was at the Treasury to see that those below the poverty level paid no income tax. It is interesting to note that the statistics about the poverty level will show that the married couple does not need twice the income of a single person to stay above the poverty level. Two cannot live as cheaply as one, but they do live more cheaply than two living separately, and this was one of the reasons for the change in the taxation of single people in 1969.

We worked on the assumption that married people live together and single people live apart, an assumption that may be inaccurate. We did not think, however, that we could determine income taxes on the basis of who was living with whom. We thought the Internal Revenue Service ought not to try to make that determination. So although the system causes some difficulty, it is based on the assumption that single people live separately and married people live together. I do not know that there is any other way for the tax system to reach a practical conclusion, except by some arbitrary adjustment.

Discussion Summary

In responding to Edwin Cohen and Joseph Minarik, June O'Neill conceded that the administrative problems associated with separate filing might make the most compelling case against her position. She noted, however, that such problems had been solved in some states and in many OECD countries.

Cohen replied that the administrative problems were not as severe at the state level, because marginal tax rates were very much lower than at the federal level. This makes it less profitable, he noted, to reallocate income and deductions artificially. He also pointed out that studying administrative problems in the United States before 1948 may be more revealing concerning the administrative difficulties associated with separate filing than would studies of European experience.

Cohen further objected to the assumption in the O'Neill paper that the wife pays the highest marginal tax rate. He asked, why not attribute the highest marginal rate to the husbands' income? Or more appropriately, why not assume that the rate brackets apply proportionately to their respective separate earnings?

O'Neill replied that the main point was, given today's conditions, it would be the wife who would pay the lower marginal rate under a separate filing system because, in the overwhelming majority of cases, the wife has the lower income. She conceded, however, that circumstances may change as women become better educated and more firmly committed to the labor force. She felt that such a change, however, would not alter the arguments for separate filing.

Geoffrey Brennan noted that the taxation of married couples provides a particularly good example of the tension between efficiency and equity. Because married women are known to have a higher labor supply elasticity than men, he pointed out that one would expect optimum tax theory to say that they should pay lower marginal tax rates on equivalent incomes. He agreed, few would accept such sex discrimination as equitable.

The Tax Treatment
of Married Couples
and the 1981 Tax Law

Daniel Feenberg

Introduction

Since the personal income tax was introduced into the United States in 1913, the selection of the taxable unit has been a source of controversy. The tax schedule has been applied to the individual, the couple, and the couple with income splitting. The choice has fluctuated over time and place, and there is still no strong societal consensus.[1]

The income tax law of 1913 specified separate filing on a single rate schedule. Separate filing has the advantage of marriage neutrality— that is, tax liabilities are not affected by the mere fact of marital status. In community property states, however, the wife had a strong legal claim to one-half of her husband's income (and vice versa), and couples in such states began to file two identical tax returns, each with one-half of the couple's income and deductions. Under a progressive tax, this tactic resulted in a lower tax liability. In 1930, the Supreme Court endorsed this procedure, and the geographic discrimination persisted until 1948.

By 1948, the tax was much heavier and much more progressive. States had begun to adopt community property legislation merely to secure for their residents the favorable treatment of income splitting on the federal tax return. In that year, Congress provided that married couples would continue to be taxed on the single schedule, but that they would pay "twice the tax on one-half the combined income." This rule persists today in several state income tax laws, and it is equivalent to the income splitting practiced by residents of community property states.

This work was supported in part by a grant from the National Science Foundation. A portion of this paper has appeared previously in "Alternative Tax Treatments of the Family," by Daniel Feenberg and Harvey Rosen (NBER working paper no. 497). Brad DeLong has provided excellent research assistance.

Income splitting was a substantial subsidy to marriage for one-earner couples and was so regarded. By 1969, the differential seemed excessive to Congress, which enacted a new schedule for single taxpayers which limited their tax to 120 percent of that for a married couple with the same taxable income. It was this law that established the current tax treatment of the married couple relative to single individuals.

Currently, single and married people face different tax schedules, with the tax liability of married individuals being based upon the couple's joint income. Consequently, tax burdens change with marital status, though one cannot predict a priori whether tax liabilities will increase or decrease when an individual marries. The answer depends in part upon the incomes of the spouses. The more similar the size of the incomes, the more likely that the "marriage tax" will be positive.

This state of affairs has been criticized for a number of reasons. Some observers, noting that the tax system often provides financial disincentives for marriage, have argued that the current regime encourages immorality.[2] Economists have tended to focus on possible inefficiencies produced when tax liability is based upon family income ("joint filing"). As Michael Boskin and Eytan Sheshinski note,[3] since the labor supply elasticities of husbands and wives differ, economic efficiency would be enhanced if their earned incomes were taxed at different rates. Yet, under a system of joint filing, spouses face the same marginal tax rate on the last dollar. A closely related criticism is that the current tax regime tends to discourage married women from entering the marketplace. This is because under joint filing the wife's tax rate is a function of the husband's earnings.

An excellent polemic against current law is provided by Lynda Moerschbraecher:

> The marriage penalty . . . serves as a disincentive to marriage, and an incentive to cohabitation, an incentive to divorce and a disincentive to reentry of the second spouse into the labor market. There is no reason for a tax provision which is not only arbitrary, but inconsistent and unintended.[4]

This author surely overstates her case. In fact, the selection of a taxable unit is controversial precisely because it is difficult. The case for marriage neutrality is admittedly compelling, but the case for horizontal equity (couples with equal family incomes should pay equal taxes) is also appealing, as is the case for progressivity in the tax schedule. Yet, these three principles are incompatible. There is, in fact, no nonnegative income tax which could provide marriage neutrality, horizontal equity, and progressivity.[5]

In a tax system with itemized deductions, separate filing does not even achieve marriage neutrality unless the "correct" allocation of deductions between the spouses can be determined. In common law states before 1948, deductions were allocated to the spouse making payment. For well-organized taxpayers this allowed deductions to be assigned in a tax-minimizing way, and it represented a departure from marriage neutrality as great as any present under the 1969 law. Deductions might plausibly be allocated in proportion to income, or split evenly, but without knowledge of the "correct" distribution, substantial nonneutrality is inevitable. An identical set of concerns relates to the disposition of dependent exemptions.

In the search for a principle to violate, the recent literature emphasizes horizontal equity as the weakest link in the paradox. The trend toward a temporary and casual style of marriage militates against the assumption of the family as an integrated consumption unit. Furthermore, the comparison between couples of equal incomes is disingenuous. They are not really equal if one couple must work twice as many hours to achieve that income. Yet it does not follow that individual filing is an equitable (or efficient) alternative. The most salient characteristic of all known tax systems is the failure to tax nonmarket goods. If all the contributions of each spouse to a marriage, both physical and spiritual, were taxed, and if marriages were made between equals in the broad sense of the term, then joint and individual filing would be the same. The failure to tax nonmarket goods is the source of the difficulty, and it is not alleviated by individual filing. The case *for* joint filing (since it may now be seen to fail to achieve horizontal equity) is weakened, however.

The 1981 tax law does respond to the apparent inequity of the marriage tax. When it takes full effect in 1983, the bill provides that 10 percent of the secondary worker's earnings (up to $30,000) shall be exempt from taxation. The child care credit is expanded to 20 percent of the first $2,400 in child or dependent care expenses for each of the taxpayer's first two dependents. The credit is increased by one point for each $2,000 that the taxpayer's income falls short of $30,000, with a maximum credit of 30 percent of expenses.[6] Together with the general rate reduction of 23 percent (only 19 percent in 1983), these charges will enhance marriage neutrality at the expense of both horizontal equity and progressivity. It cannot be expected, therefore, to be the last legislative initiative on this subject.

The purpose of this paper is to show the magnitude and distribution of the marriage tax under both the current and the new tax laws and to show careful estimates of the effect on revenues, labor supply, and welfare of the introduction of the secondary earner's exemption and the liberalization of the child care credit.

The section on static simulations shows how the distribution and magnitude of the marriage tax burden (or benefit) are changed by the new tax law, under the assumption of no behavioral response. Although static simulations showing the distribution of burden for the marriage tax have been provided by Emil Sunley,[7] he does not indicate the source of the data. The labor force behavior of married women is quite responsive to the net wage.[8] Thus, ignoring the labor supply responses of married women is likely to lead to biased estimates of the effects of tax reform proposals. The simulations reported in the section on results explicitly incorporate endogenous work decisions for wives.

Unfortunately, even a rather complete set of variables relating to a household's tax situation does not include all the information needed to predict the effects of taxes on labor supply. Standard theoretical considerations, for example, suggest that an important determinant of labor supply is the wage rate, but it is not available on any of our data sets. Another section (on methodological issues in behavioral simulation) of this paper outlines our approach to the problem of imputing such missing data. A more detailed discussion is given in a work coauthored with Harvey Rosen.[9]

A later section of the paper describes the behavioral assumptions (specified in a utility-theoretic format) for the simulations presented in the section on results. The trusting reader may proceed directly from the section on static simulations to the section on results without confusion.

Static Simulations

As noted previously, the distribution and the size of the marriage tax depend largely upon the distribution of income between spouses, the degree of progressivity of the tax schedules, the personal exemption, and the difference between the single and joint schedules. A host of other provisions in the law also play at least a minimum role.

The most important of these other provisions, and the only one that the Current Population Survey (CPS) data allow us to account for, is the earned income credit (EIC). The EIC provides a refundable credit of 10 percent of wages and salaries, but not more than $500, and only to individuals or couples with dependents. The credit vanishes gradually as income exceeds $5,000 and vanishes completely at $10,000. Because the income limits for the take-back are independent of marital status, the EIC is the major source of marriage tax burden in low- to moderate-income households.

Other sources of nonneutrality in 1979 include the capital loss limits ($3,000 single or joint), the zero-bracket amount ($2,300 for single returns but only $3,400 for joint returns), the child care credit

35

($960 maximum for everyone), the minimum tax on preferences (a $10,000 offset is independent of marital status), and the alternative minimum tax on preferences, which is a progressive tax (rates from 0.1 to 0.25) on which income splitting is not allowed.

Data. The March 1980 Current Population Survey serves as the basic data source for the static (no behavioral response) simulations in this section. It is a good source because it is fairly recent, reflecting 1979 income levels. It is representative of the entire U.S. population, and it includes separate income information for husbands and wives. Other possible surveys include husbands' and wives' labor income separately but not their property income. Even here there is some ambiguity over the intrafamily distribution of property income. The CPS data do not pretend to represent what individual property income would have been had the couple not married, or even what it would be if the couple divorced. It is merely the subjective allocation made by the respondent under a tax law which is neutral with respect to distribution. Under a nonneutral tax the distribution might be quite different.

The chief disadvantage of the CPS is the lack of any information on itemized deductions, but it is also true that CPS property income corresponds poorly with tax return data. Lastly, income items are truncated at $50,000, which affects the top 3 percent of husbands but essentially no wives. No adjustment has been made to the income data, but an imputed value of deductible expense has been assumed.[10] More sophisticated procedures for imputing data are suggested in the section on methodological issues in behavioral simulation and are applied, in the section on results, to a tax return data set.

Where 1983 income levels are required, they are obtained from a projected *nominal* per capita income growth factor of 1.49 for 1979 to 1983. This corresponds closely with both administration and Congressional Budget Office projections. The disagreement among forecasters applies mostly to the decomposition of income growth into real and price-level components. The actual calculation of tax owed is done by a suite of FORTRAN programs known as TAXSIM which are maintained by the author at the National Bureau of Economic Research.

The Distribution of the Marriage Tax. In table 1, the average marriage tax is given for each of several combinations of spouses' adjusted gross income. The law applied is that current in 1979–1981, and the income levels are those for 1979.[11] The marriage tax is defined as the difference between the tax due on separate filings using the individual income items, and the tax due on a joint return. Deductions and exemptions are allocated in proportion to income. This allocation is fairly crucial in

TABLE 1

PERCENTAGE OF MARRIED COUPLES, BY INCOME OF EACH SPOUSE (%), AND AVERAGE MARRIAGE PENALTY ($), 1979

Husband's Income ($)	Wife's Income ($)				
	0–5,000	5,000–10,000	10,000–20,000	20,000–30,000	30,000+
0–10,000	16.4%	5.8%	3.2%	0.3%	<0.1%
	−2	226	22	−187	−2,680
10,000–20,000	21.1%	9.1%	6.9%	0.4%	0.1%
	−290	406	525	1,040	1,090
20,000–30,000	15.2%	4.5%	4.0%	0.5%	0.1%
	−734	321	869	1,920	2,900
30,000–40,000	4.2%	1.0%	1.0%	0.3%	0.1%
	−1,380	158	1,170	2,460	3,140
40,000–50,000	1.8%	0.3%	0.3%	0.1%	<0.1%
	−2,180	−305	1,070	2,770	4,390
	2.2%	0.4%	0.4%	0.1%	0.1%
50,000+	−2,880	−217	628	2,570	4,640

NOTE: A minus sign (−) indicates a bonus. Figures not followed by a percent sign (%) are dollar amounts.
SOURCE: Current Population Survey, March 1980, and TAXSIM.

determining the results. If a tax-minimizing distribution of deductions is allowed, the estimated penalties are substantially larger.

The table clearly shows the tendency of the penalty to increase with joint income and to decrease with income inequality. The relative rarity of high-income women produces sufficient inequality to make the preponderant marriage tax negative—that is, to make it a bonus—as will be seen in a later table.

Figure 1 gives us an alternative mode of presentation. The contours show lines of equal marriage penalty in the spouses' income space. The same law is applied as for table 1. To produce a three-dimensional plot, however, several additional assumptions must be made. There are assumed to be no children (this includes 17 million of the 41 million couples), deductions are assumed to be 20 percent of adjusted gross income (AGI), and income is assumed to be labor income for the purpose of maximum tax. The same pattern emerges as in table 1 but with perhaps greater clarity. Each contour is labeled with the percentage

FIGURE 1

PERCENTAGE OF MARRIED COUPLES, WITHOUT CHILDREN, WHO PAID PENALTY, BY INCOME OF EACH SPOUSE,
AND THE AMOUNT OF TAX ($), 1979

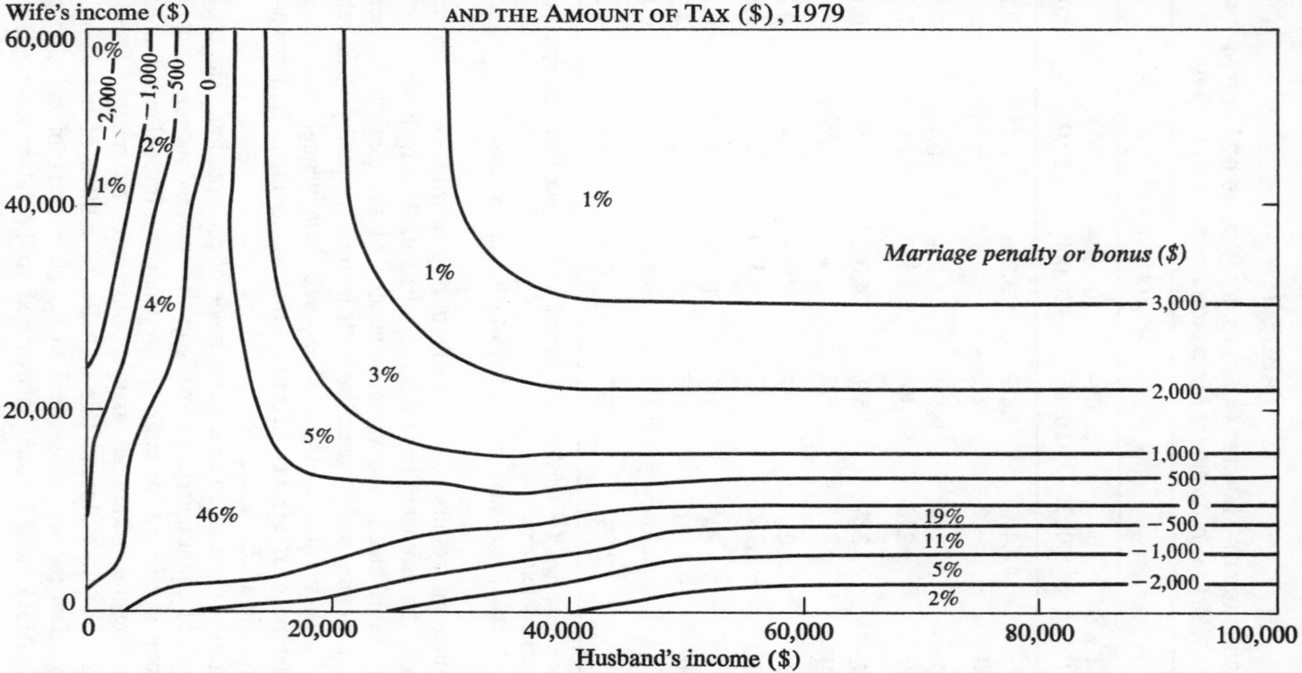

Wife's income ($)

60,000

40,000

20,000

0

0%   0
      −500
      −1,000
      −2,000

2%

1%

1%

1%

3%

5%

46%

4%

Marriage penalty or bonus ($)

3,000

2,000

1,000
500
0
−500
−1,000
−2,000

19%
11%
5%
2%

0   20,000   40,000   60,000   80,000   100,000

Husband's income ($)

NOTE: The contour plot shows lines of equal marriage penalty. Each line is labeled at the far right with the amount of penalty (negative values for a marriage bonus). If the wife's income is $30,000, for example, and the husband's income is $40,000 to $60,000, the penalty is about $3,000. The contours are symmetric about a 45 percent line through the origin, so the husband's and wife's incomes may be interchanged. Each connected region of the graph is labeled with the percentage of childless couples whose incomes place them in that region. One percent, for example, pay a penalty of $3,000 or more. Some of the regions are disconnected: for example, 23 percent (= 19 percent + 4 percent) of the joint returns show a benefit of zero to $500.

38

of childless couples who did fall into that category, given the assumed deductions. Table 2 provides cumulative distributions of the marriage penalty and bonus for 1979. From column 2 we see that substantial penalties (over $500) were not unusual, being present in 14.5 percent of the cases, but that a bonus of this size was somewhat more likely and went to 23.3 percent of couples in the sample.

The secondary earner's deduction (SED) enacted in 1981 takes full effect in 1983, when it provides for a deduction, not to exceed $3,000, of 10 percent of the secondary worker's earnings. By 1983, a general tax cut of 19 percent will also be in effect, and changes in nominal income will also substantially affect real tax liabilities. Table 3 repeats table 1, but at 1983 income levels, and with 1983 tax rates without the secondary earner's deduction (second line in each cell) and with it (third line). The second and third lines in the cells along the top row and the left-hand column show little change, but the marriage penalty in most of the other cells is substantially reduced with the SED. Figure 2 shows the hypothetical marriage penalty for 1983 in the absence of any SED. Figure 3 shows the contours of equal marriage tax amelioration, and figure 4 shows the final situation, including the SED.

Figures 5 and 6 repeat figures 3 and 4 but with contours of equivalent fractions of income paid in marriage penalty. In figure 5 we see that 11 percent of 1983 households would pay a penalty of 2 percent or more of family income without the SED, but that this would happen only in the case of rather well-off couples. Figure 6 shows the situation with the enacted law, in which case only 2 percent of couples are so abused, and so on. It should be clear from these figures that any reduction in the marriage penalty is obtained at the expense of progressivity. Although this paper makes no attempt to balance these competing virtues, it does try to emphasize the competition between them.

Table 4 shows the cumulative distribution of penalty and bonus for 1983 for all couples, with and without the secondary earner's deduction. The last two columns of the table show the amount of penalty or bonus and the mean change in tax revenue due to the deduction for those couples in the indicated penalty or bonus categories *without the deduction*. Without the deduction there is a reduction in marriage bonus from $14.5 billion in 1979 (see table 2) to $13.0 billion in 1983. Gross marriage penalty, however, increases slightly from $9.0 billion to $9.3 billion. The overall reduction in absolute deviations is $1.2 billion. The introduction of an SED reduces the marriage penalty by $2 billion to $7.3 billion, but it increases the marriage bonus by $1.7 billion to $14.7 billion. The net improvement in absolute deviations of $0.3 billion is small relative to the improvement associated with the 1981 law's general reduction in progressivity.

FIGURE 2

PERCENTAGE OF MARRIED COUPLES, WITHOUT CHILDREN AND WITHOUT THE SECONDARY INCOME DEDUCTION,
EXPECTED TO PAY PENALTY, BY INCOME OF EACH SPOUSE, AND THE AMOUNT OF TAX ($), 1983

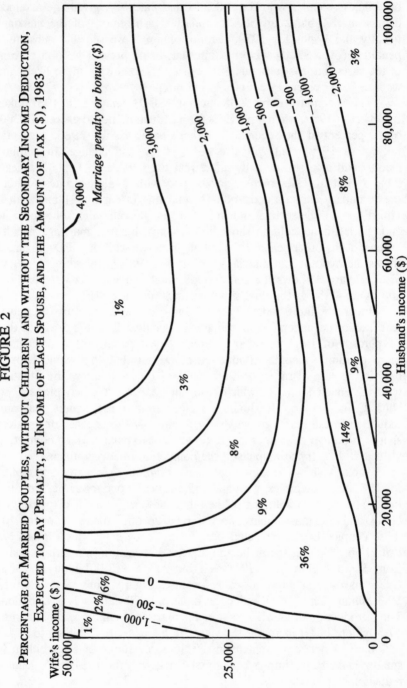

NOTE: Contour lines are labeled with the amount of marriage penalty. Negative values indicate a bonus. Also see note for figure 1.

FIGURE 3

TAX RELIEF GIVEN TO MARRIED COUPLES, WITHOUT CHILDREN, AS A RESULT OF THE SECONDARY INCOME DEDUCTION, 1983

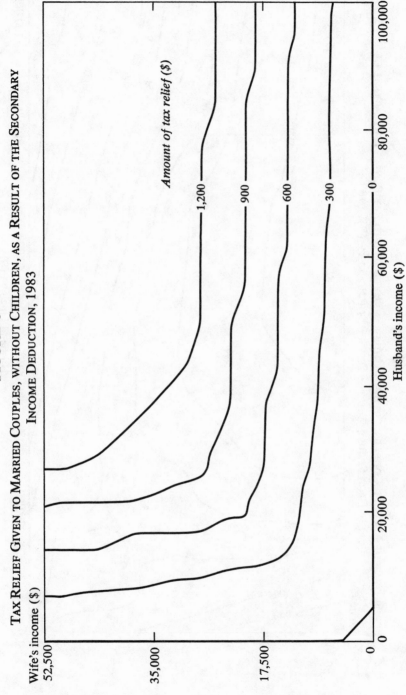

41

42

FIGURE 4

PERCENTAGE OF MARRIED COUPLES, WITHOUT CHILDREN, EXPECTED TO PAY PENALTY, BY INCOME OF
EACH SPOUSE, AND THE AMOUNT OF PENALTY ($), 1983

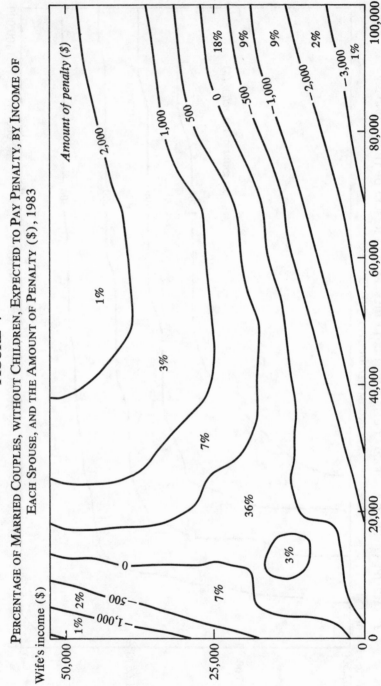

NOTE: Contour lines are labeled with the amount of marriage penalty. Negative values indicate a bonus. Also see note for figure 1.

FIGURE 5

PERCENTAGE OF MARRIED COUPLES, WITHOUT CHILDREN AND WITHOUT SECONDARY INCOME DEDUCTION, EXPECTED TO PAY PENALTY, BY INCOME OF EACH SPOUSE, AND THE PENALTY PAID AS A FRACTION OF INCOME, 1983

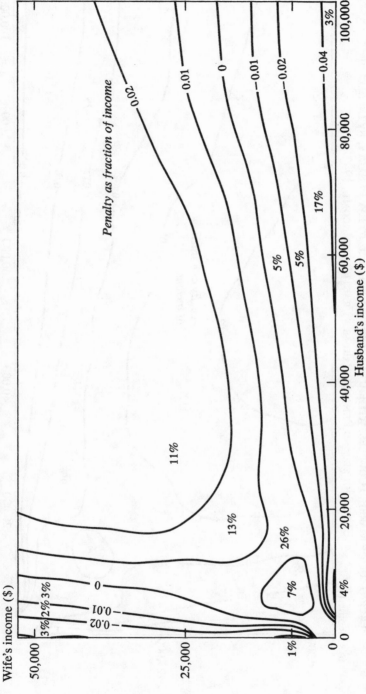

NOTE: Contour lines are labeled with the penalty paid as a fraction of income. Negative values indicate a bonus. Also see note for figure 1.

43

44

FIGURE 6

PERCENTAGE OF MARRIED COUPLES, WITHOUT CHILDREN, EXPECTED TO PAY PENALTY, BY INCOME OF EACH SPOUSE, AND PENALTY PAID AS A FRACTION OF INCOME, 1983

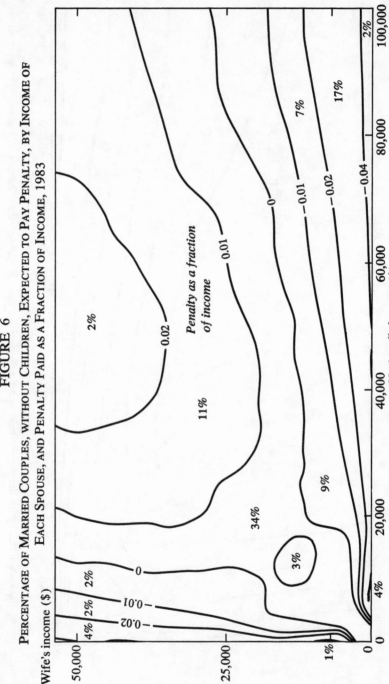

NOTE: Contour lines are labeled with the penalty paid as a fraction of income. Negative values indicate a bonus. Also see note for figure 1.

TABLE 2
MARRIAGE PENALTY FOR ALL COUPLES, 1979

Marriage Penalty or Bonus ($)	Percentage of All Returns	Cumulative Percentage of Returns	Penalty Paid or Bonus Received ($ billions)
Less than −4,000	0.4	0.04	−0.7
−4,000 to −3,000	0.9	1.3	−0.9
−3,000 to −2,000	2.5	3.8	−2.2
−2,000 to −1,000	8.2	12.0	−4.5
−1,000 to −500	11.3	23.3	−3.4
−500 to 0	25.8	49.1	−2.8
Subtotal for bonus			−14.5
0	5.8	54.9	0
0 to 500	30.6	85.5	3.3
500 to 1,000	9.5	94.0	2.6
1,000 to 2,000	4.6	98.6	1.9
2,000 to 3,000	0.9	99.5	0.7
3,000 to 4,000	0.4	99.9	0.3
Greater than 4,000	<0.1	100.0	0.3
Subtotal for penalty			9.0

NOTE: A minus sign (−) indicates a bonus. The number of joint returns in 1978 was 41,400,000.
SOURCE: Current Population Survey, March 1980, and TAXSIM.

The last two columns show that this generally poor result occurs in spite of the fact that $3.2 billion in reductions goes to couples who would otherwise be paying a penalty, and only $0.4 billion to those receiving a bonus. The SED's greatest effect is to move couples from the penalty category to the bonus category. It does not succeed in reducing the extent of nonneutrality induced by joint filing.

Methodological Issues in Behavioral Simulation

A behavioral simulation requires data on individuals' tax situations and on their economic and demographic characteristics. The tax information is required to make careful predictions of the revenue implications of alternative tax regimes. The economic and demographic information is needed to estimate the impact of tax changes upon economic behavior.

The fundamental methodological problems of this study are consequences of the fact that no publicly available data set has all this information. The March CPS, though rich in income data, does not show

TABLE 3

PERCENTAGE OF MARRIED COUPLES, BY INCOME OF EACH SPOUSE,
AND AVERAGE MARRIAGE PENALTY ($), WITH AND WITHOUT
SECONDARY EARNER'S DEDUCTION

Husband's Income ($)	Wife's Income ($)				
	0–5,000	5,000–10,000	10,000–20,000	20,000–30,000	30,000+
0–10,000	8.3%	3.1%	3.4%	0.8%	0.2%
	−18	200	−43	−432	−822
	−22	169	−89	−471	−871
10,000–20,000	11.9%	5.0%	6.3%	1.1%	0.2%
	−287	377	603	934	1,190
	−298	255	331	598	702
20,000–30,000	13.0%	4.1%	6.5%	2.2%	0.3%
	−738	310	871	1,730	2,500
	−754	139	474	1,050	1,690
30,000–40,000	9.6%	2.7%	3.3%	1.2%	0.4%
	−1,250	200	1,110	2,330	3,290
	−1,270	−8	627	1,460	2,300
40,000–50,000	4.6%	0.9%	1.5%	0.6%	0.3%
	−1,720	7	1,120	2,590	3,560
	−1,730	7	1,120	2,590	2,650
50,000+	5.2%	1.0%	1.3%	0.7%	0.5%
	−3,240	−1,090	572	2,060	3,870
	−3,240	−1,250	209	1,300	2,980

NOTE: The first number in each cell represents the percentage of couples in that income category. The second number is the mean marriage penalty paid without the secondary earner's deduction. The third number is the mean marriage penalty paid with the secondary earner's deduction. Negative numbers indicate a bonus. Figures not followed by a percent sign (%) are dollar amounts.

SOURCE: Current Population Survey, March 1980, and TAXSIM.

the wage rate, which is asked in May. It also does not give any suitable hours-last-year variable, though hours-last-week data are available. The data sources typically used by economists to estimate behavioral equations have virtually no federal income tax data.[12] Data sets that are rich in tax information, however, tend to tell us little else about members of the sample. Because individuals do not report wage rates and hours of work on their federal income tax returns, TAXSIM has no information on these crucial magnitudes. Clearly then, one must bring together

TABLE 4

MARRIAGE PENALTY AND BONUS FOR ALL COUPLES, WITH AND WITHOUT SECONDARY EARNER'S DEDUCTION, 1983
(1979 dollars)

Marriage Penalty or Bonus ($)	Without Secondary Earner's Deduction			With Secondary Earner's Deduction			Amount Based on Prededuction Brackets ($ billions)	Mean Change in Tax Revenue ($ billions)
	Percentage of returns	Cumulative percentage of returns	Amount of penalty or bonus ($ billions)	Percentage of returns	Cumulative percentage of returns	Amount of penalty or bonus		
Less than −4,000	0.1	0.1	0.5	0.2	0.2	−0.8	−0.6	32
−4,000 to −3,000	0.3	0.4	−0.4	0.4	0.6	−0.5	−0.4	23
−3,000 to −2,000	1.9	2.3	−1.9	2.2	2.8	−2.1	−1.9	21
−2,000 to −1,000	6.5	8.8	−3.6	6.5	9.3	−3.7	−3.6	9
−1,000 to −500	12.8	21.6	−3.7	13.2	22.5	−4.0	−3.7	6
−500 to 0	26.5	48.1	−2.8	30.4	52.9	−3.7	−2.3	46
Subtotal for bonus			−13.0			−14.7	−13.4	
0	5.9	54.0	0	6.2	59.1	0	0.2	71
0 to 500	31	85.1	3.2	28.2	87.3	2.7	1.8	130
500 to 1,000	11.1	96.1	3.1	9.6	96.9	2.6	2.2	190
1,000 to 2,000	3.0	99.1	1.7	2.7	99.6	1.2	1.1	470
2,000 to 3,000	0.5	99.6	0.5	0.3	99.9	0.4	0.4	550
3,000 to 4,000	0.2	99.8	0.3	0.1	100	0.2	0.2	590
Greater than 4,000	0.2	100	0.2	<0.1	100	0.1	0.2	1,300
Subtotal for penalty			9.3			7.3	6.1	

NOTE: A minus sign (−) indicates a bonus.
SOURCE: Current Population Survey, March 1980, and TAXSIM.

information from (at least) two different data sources in order to perform tax simulations with endogenous labor supply responses.

A popular technique for combining information is statistical matching.[13] The first step in this procedure is to isolate a set of variables common to both data sets. A search is then made to determine which observations of each data set are "close" on the basis of these variables.[14] The close observations are pooled to form a "synthetic" observation, which is then treated as if it were generated by a single behavioral unit. Here we outline as an alternative an inexpensive imputation procedure which provides the promise of consistent estimates of revenue effects.

Predicting Tax Revenues. Let y be a vector of variables endogenous to the tax system. Included are items such as taxable income, which depends directly upon provisions of the tax code, and variables such as pretax earnings, which depend upon the tax system only to the extent that the latter influences economic behavior. Let x be a vector of exogenous variables such as age or (in this study) property income. If the tax code at a given time is represented by the parameter **B,** then we can think of the tax system as a function t (**x,y,B**) which determines the amount of taxes owed by an individual given the relevant exogenous and endogenous variables. Our problem is to determine how revenues change when there is a change from the current tax regime, denoted **B′**, to some new tax regime, **B″**.

We shall call the distribution of the exogenous and endogenous variables in the population $f(\mathbf{x,y} \mid \mathbf{B'})$. Then total tax revenue T under the current regime **B′** is

$$T(\mathbf{B'}) = N \int\mathbf{x} \int\mathbf{y}\, t(\mathbf{x,y,B'})f(\mathbf{x,y} \mid \mathbf{B'})d\mathbf{y}d\mathbf{x} \qquad (1)$$

where N is the total number of taxpaying units.

The analytic integration implied by equation 1 cannot in practice be performed. An obvious alternative is its discrete analogue

$$\hat{T}(\mathbf{B'}) = N \sum_{i=1}^{I} t(x_i, y_i, \mathbf{B'})P_i \qquad (2)$$

where y_i and x_i $(i = 1, \ldots, I)$ are I sample observations from the universe of N taxpaying units, and P_i is one over the probability of the observation being included in the sample.

Under tax regime **B″** tax revenues are

$$T(\mathbf{B''}) = \int\mathbf{x} \int\mathbf{y}\, t(\mathbf{x}, \mathbf{y}, B'')f(\mathbf{x}, \mathbf{y} \mid \mathbf{B''})d\mathbf{y}d\mathbf{x} \qquad (3)$$

Unfortunately, even knowledge of $f(\mathbf{x,y} \mid \mathbf{B'})$ does not in general give us $f(\mathbf{x,y} \mid \mathbf{B''})$, the joint distribution of **x** and **y** under the new regime. Only with the restrictive assumption that $\mathbf{y}$ is inelastic with respect to the change in tax regimes can we estimate new tax revenues as

$$\hat{T}(\mathbf{B}'') = \sum_{i=1}^{I} t(\mathbf{x}, \mathbf{y}, \mathbf{B}'')P_i \qquad (4)$$

For changes in tax regimes of the sort being analyzed in this paper, the assumption of exogenism is too strong.

If $\mathbf{y}$ is known to be some stochastic function of the $\mathbf{x}$'s, then one is tempted to replace the y's with their predicted values

$$T(\mathbf{B}'') = \sum_{i=1}^{I} t(\mathbf{x}, \mathbf{y}(\mathbf{x},\mathbf{B}''), \mathbf{B}'')\,P_i \qquad (5)$$

but a much better procedure adds the prediction error under the known regime back to the new predicted $\mathbf{y}$

$$T(\mathbf{B}'') = \sum_{i=1}^{I} t(\mathbf{x}, \mathbf{y}(\mathbf{x},\mathbf{B}'')) + (\mathbf{y} - \mathbf{y}(\mathbf{x}, \mathbf{B}'), \mathbf{B}'')\,P_i \qquad (6)$$

Of course, the discussion so far has ignored the possibility that some variables in the $\mathbf{x}$ or $\mathbf{y}$ vectors may be missing from the TAXSIM file.

Imputing Base Line Data. Most plausible theories of labor supply suggest that it is necessary to know something about individuals' wage rates and hours of work in order to predict how alternative tax regimes affect revenues. Federal tax returns, however, include only the product of hours and the wage rate—that is, earnings. In this section we show how information from the University of Michigan Panel Survey of Income Dynamics (PSID) concerning the joint distribution of earning hours can be used in conjunction with tax return data to impute the missing data. The PSID was chosen because it is the only data set we could locate that includes both wage rate and annual income data for a sample of the U.S. population. The major disadvantage of the PSID is the paucity of families in higher-income brackets.

The first step is to use data from the 1975 survey year (which is based on income and hours in 1974) to estimate a regression of the wife's wage as some function of those variables common to the PSID and TAXSIM. The set of common variables consists of wife's earnings, husband's earnings, a dummy variable to indicate whether the wife is over sixty-five, and the number of exemptions. A regression of the wife's wage on her own earnings may seem strange. Since earnings are the product of hours and the wage rate, they are an endogenous variable. This observation, though correct, is still beside the point. The purpose of the equation is not to estimate a structural equation, but merely to

49

describe the conditional distribution of the wife's wage rate on the common variables.

The actual imputation applies the coefficient from the extraneous regression to the data in the TAXSIM model. To the conditional mean wage implied by the regression is added a random selection from the set of residuals.

The key assumption for this procedure to be correct is that, *conditional* on the common variables, the wife's wage rate must be linearly independent of the other variables in the model. This seems quite reasonable because once we know earnings, and so on, knowing the wage rate probably contributes little to predicting taxable income. Assuming an independent wage rate for the wife is not *necessarily* true. It may be that extensive deductions are associated with high reservation wages, *ceteris paribus*. This would generate conditional dependence between the true value of the imputed variable and another variable in the model which would not be reflected in the imputation. The presence of such dependence, however, cannot be tested. Any data set with which the assumption might be tested would be a candidate for the simulation itself and would obviate the need for the imputation procedure. In the absence of such dependence the synthetic data set will display the correct variance-covariance structure and the simulations will not be biased by the presence of error in the imputed variable. A more detailed justification and a complete specification for the imputation are contained in Feenberg and Rosen.[15]

Of course, for nonworking wives this procedure could not be implemented because of the need for a wage variable to serve as a regressand. Instead, a procedure was followed similar to that suggested by Hall.[16] We estimated for the sample of working wives a regression of the wage rate on husband's income, number of dependents, and an over-sixty-five dummy variable, and used the results to impute wages to the nonworkers. As is well known, this procedure does not correct for the possible effects of selectivity bias.[17] Given our paucity of explanatory variables, it seemed to us pretentious to attempt this rather subtle correction. Moreover, Hausman has pointed out that in cases like ours, the correction usually makes no practical difference anyway.[18]

Behavioral Assumptions

We now turn to the question of how, given our figures on wages, rates, and hours of work, we can simulate the effects of various tax changes on work effort and the distribution of family income. In effect, our task is to specify the function that relates hours of work to exogenous variables and the tax code. The framework used is the standard microeconomic theory of the leisure income choice.[19] The theory views the hours of work decision as an outcome when the individual maximizes a utility function subject to a budget constraint. We shall first discuss the budget constraint generated by the personal income tax system and then explain how preferences are modeled.

The Budget Constraint. Let us first consider the budget constraint faced by an untaxed individual with wage w and unearned income I. The constraint can be represented graphically on a diagram with income plotted on the vertical axis and hours of leisure on the horizontal axis. In figure 7, if the individual's time endowment is OT hours, then the budget constraint is a straight line MN, with slope $-w$ and vertical intercept $I (= TN)$. Behind the linear budget constraint are the assumptions that the fixed costs associated with working are negligible and that the gross wage does not vary with hours of work. These assumptions are common to most studies of labor supply. Although the consequences of relaxing them have been discussed,[20] there is no agreement on whether they are important empirically. In this study, we retain the conventional assumption that the pretax budget constraint can be represented as a straight line.

Let us now assume that the individual is subjected to a proportional tax on both earned income and unearned income. Then the effective budget constraint facing the individual in figure 7 is PQ, with the tax rate being NP/NT. Even with such a simple tax system, one would have to know both the uncompensated elasticity of hours with respect to the wage and the income elasticity in order to predict the effect of taxes upon hours of work.

Of course, the U.S. tax system is progressive with respect to taxable income, not proportional. As an individual's income bracket changes, she generally faces a discrete increase in the marginal tax rate. This leads to a kinked budget constraint like $RSUVW$ in figure 8. If the individual's optimum is along, say, segment US, then she behaves *exactly* as if she were optimizing along a linear budget constraint with the same slope as US but with intercept W'. This fact, which has been observed by Hall and others, is extremely useful because it allows us to characterize the individual's opportunities as a series of straight lines.[21] The distance TR' will be referred to as "effective" nonlabor income.

Included in the tax code are a complicated set of exemptions, deductions, and credits. Conceptually, it is not difficult to include their effects in the budget constraint—all that is required is that we be able to compute net income at any given number of hours of work. It should be noted, however, that some tax provisions actually lead to nonconvexities in that there may be several points at which indifference curves are

FIGURE 7
BUDGET CONSTRAINTS ON AN INDIVIDUAL

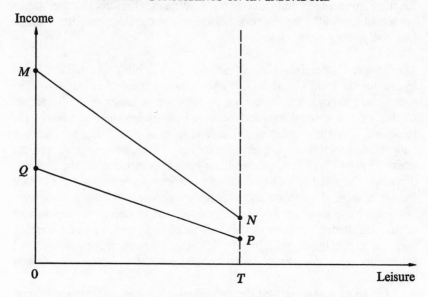

FIGURE 8
A KINKED BUDGET CONSTRAINT

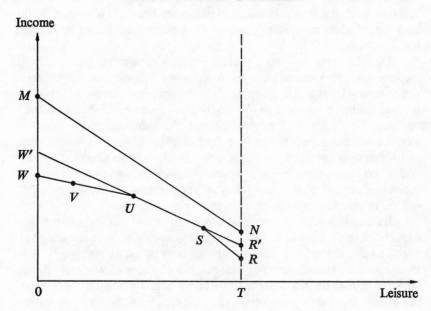

52

tangent to the budget constraint in order to find a global maximum. The specification of a complete utility function—not just a labor supply curve —thus becomes a necessity.

Functional form. The standard static theory of labor supply behavior starts with a family utility function which depends upon family income and the amounts of leisure time consumed by each spouse. The labor supply of each spouse depends upon the net wages of *both* spouses and effective unearned income. Using several fairly reasonable assumptions, however, one can specify a family utility function with only two arguments: wife's leisure and net family income. This simplification is permissible if the husband's labor supply is perfectly inelastic. In fact, many econometric studies of the labor supply behavior of married men have tended to show that both wage [22] effects and income effects are small in absolute value.[23] We therefore adopt the simpler model as a reasonable first approximation to reality.

Now that we have decided upon the arguments for the utility function, we turn to the question of its functional form. In making a selection, two criteria are important: (1) It should be simple, both to limit computational costs and to facilitate intuitive understanding of the results; and (2) it should be fairly broadly consistent with econometric estimates of labor supply.

Recently, Hausman has suggested that one way to satisfy these criteria is to start with a labor supply function that fits the data fairly well and then take advantage of duality theory to find the underlying (indirect) utility function.[24] More specifically, Hausman observes that the linear labor supply function has proved very useful in explaining labor supply behavior.

$$H = aw + bA + s \qquad (7)$$

where H is annual hours of work, w is the net wage, A is effective income, and a, b, and s are parameters. Using Roy's Identity, which relates various derivatives of the indirect utility function to H, Hausman shows that the indirect utility function, $v(w,A)$, underlying equation 7 is

$$v(w,A) = A + (a/b)w - a/b^2 + (s/b)e^{bw} \qquad (8)$$

Given the ranges over which a particular individual's w and A will vary in our simulations, equations 7 and 8 seem to be adequate approximations, and they are adapted for use in this paper. We assign each family a set of utility function parameters calculated so that current behavior is perfectly predicted by equation 1. Specifically, we assume that the hours elasticity with respect to the wage for the ith family is A_i. Then a_i, b_i, and s_i are the solutions to the system.[25]

$$w_i = (w_i/H_i)a_i \tag{9a}$$

$$A_i = (w_i/H_i)b_i \tag{9b}$$

$$s_i = H_i - a_i w_i - b_i A_i \tag{9c}$$

Elasticity estimates. In order to solve equations 9a–9c, we require estimates of wage and unearned income elasticities for married women. The literature suggests fairly high values for the wage elasticity. The studies reviewed by Heckman and others report values between 0.2 and 1.35, and some investigators have proposed even larger estimates.[26] There is virtually no guidance with respect to how the wage elasticity varies with income level. Indeed, due to the thinness of all statistical samples in very high income groups (that is, family income greater than $35,000 in 1974) essentially *nothing* is known about the labor supply response of the women at the top end of the scale. Nor is anything known about the effect of the number of dependents on the price or income elasticities, though the presence of small children is known to reduce mean labor supply dramatically. We use a conservative value of 0.5 in this paper.

With respect to η_A we find that here also the literature provides less than firm guidance. This is due in part to the problems involved in measuring correctly family unearned income. (Difficulties arise because of underreporting, estimating imputed income from durable goods, and so on.) In addition, unearned income is usually treated as an exogenous variable in hours equations, though in a life cycle context it would be endogenous. Heckman and Killingsworth report that most investigators have found values of η_A between -0.002 and -2.0. We use -0.1 in our simulations.

The demand side of the labor market is not modeled. That is, it is assumed that the wage rate offered to married women will not be affected by the increase in supply. Given the small change in hours induced by the tax change relative to total hours in the economy, this is appropriate.

Welfare effects. Given the explicit indirect utility function (equation 8), it is relatively straightforward to calculate a compensating or equivalent variation for the change in tax rates. We choose the equivalent variation as our measure of welfare loss. It is defined as the sum of money necessary to restore an individual to his original utility level, evaluated at the original prices. That is, EV is defined by the implicit equation $v(w_0, A_1 + EV) = v(w_1, A_1)$, which evaluates to

$$EV = e^{b(w_1 - w_0)} (A_1 + (a/b)w_1 - a/b^2 + a/b)$$
$$- (A_1 + (a/b)w_0 - a/b^2 + a/b)$$

The difference between the *EV* and the revenue loss of the change is an exact measure of dead-weight loss.[27] The use of the Marshallian measure (the area under the labor supply curve between w_1 and w_0 minus the revenue loss) would not be justified. Though the Marshallian consumer surplus measure is ordinarily an excellent approximation to the compensating or equivalent variation,[28] the same result does not hold for the corresponding measure of dead-weight loss.[29] The absolute error inherent in Marshall's measure of dead-weight loss is the same as the error in his measure of consumer surplus, but relative to the smaller base the percentage error may be much larger.

Results

There are, of course, an essentially unlimited number of ways in which the tax treatment of the family could be modified. The effects of a number of alternatives, including voluntary or compulsory separate filing and a secondary earner's credit, are evaluated in Feenberg and Rosen.[30] In this paper only the reforms enacted in the 1981 tax law are discussed.

Each tax regime naturally induces a change in revenue collections. It is possible that in practice legislators might want to introduce additional taxes to keep revenues constant, or they might finance a tax reduction with bonds or money. One cannot know in advance, however, what form these adjustments might take or what effects they might have. In the light of this ambiguity we have not attempted any equal revenue comparisons.

The base line data in table 5 are taken from a stratified random sample of tax returns taken from the U.S. Treasury 1974 Tax Model. The subsample includes one in forty joint returns with nonworking wives and one in twenty joint returns for couples with working wives. The data are extrapolated to reflect 1979 totals (the extrapolation to 1983 seemed too extreme), and the 1979 tax law is applied. The table shows adjusted gross income, federal income tax liability, marginal tax rates on earned income, and the imputed hours of work per year for the wives. Generally, average and marginal tax rates rise with AGI class. The number of hours worked tends to rise with income, but the relationship is not strictly increasing. As other family income increases, there is an income effect which would decrease the number of hours that wives work if, as expected, leisure is a normal good. There is also a tendency, however, for the wife's pretax wage to be positively correlated with other family income, which encourages work in the market (assuming a positively sloped supply-of-hours schedule). One cannot say a priori which effect will dominate.

TABLE 5

AVERAGE HOURS WORKED BY WIVES, BY INCOME CLASS AND
TAX STATUS, 1979
(joint returns)

AGI Class ($)	Number of Returns (1,000s)	Average AGI ($)	Tax Liability ($)	Marginal Tax Rate	Hours Worked per Year
Less than 5,000	1,676	2,862	24	−0.04	102
5,000–10,000	4,180	7,789	123	0.15	331
10,000–15,000	5,744	12,580	873	0.17	501
15,000–20,000	7,168	17,390	1,799	0.23	517
20,000–30,000	12,648	24,450	3,248	0.28	779
30,000–50,000	10,483	37,370	6,543	0.33	1,000
50,000–100,000	2,877	65,000	16,290	0.47	741
Greater than 100,000	571	171,600	65,130	0.53	681
Mean		26,908	4,678	0.26	681
Total	45,300	1.2×10^{11}	2.1×10^{11}		3.1×10^{10}

SOURCE: U.S. Treasury 1974 Tax Model and TAXSIM.

Secondary Earner's Deduction. Table 6 shows the effects of allowing the family to deduct 10 percent of the first $30,000 of the secondary worker's earnings from taxable income. A wage elasticity of hours with respect to the net wage of 0.5 is assumed. In order to maintain comparability with table 5, the adjusted gross income classes are those associated with the status quo.

The secondary earner's deduction has a modest effect on labor supply. Compared with table 5, table 6 shows that, on average, wives supply fifteen more hours worked per year. The increase is most marked in the $30,000–50,000 range, where the combination of a relatively high marginal tax rate and labor force participation rate increases the effect.

On the average, tax collections fall by about $72 (out of $4,602), and the decrease is greater in the higher brackets. For the sake of comparison we have noted in the second column of table 6 what the revenue predictions would have been had we postulated perfectly inelastic labor supplies for wives. The table suggests that about one-third of the revenue loss is restored by the increased tax base associated with the higher labor supply. Although this is considerably short of the claims of some that reductions in rates will be self-financing, it is significant

TABLE 6

SECONDARY EARNER'S DEDUCTION AND ITS EFFECT ON
HOURS WORKED AND WELFARE COSTS, 1979

| AGI Class ($) | Tax Liability | | Marginal Tax Rate | Hours Worked | Change in Dead-Weight Loss ($) |
	Exogenous behavior ($)	$\eta_w = 0.5$ ($)			
Less than 5,000	24	25	−0.039	102	−1.34
5,000–10,000	120	121	0.15	332	−0.81
10,000–15,000	852	854	0.17	504	−2.7
15,000–20,000	1,767	1,773	0.17	524	−9.3
20,000–30,000	3,161	3,183	0.26	798	−30.5
30,000–50,000	6,306	6,369	0.31	1,028	−180
50,000–100,000	15,960	16,110	0.45	773	−168
Greater than 100,000	65,010	65,080	0.52	506	−606
Mean	4,570	4,603	0.25	697	−46
Total	2.073×10^{11}	2.087×10^{11}		3.16×10^{10}	-2.09×10^{9}

SOURCE: U.S. Treasury 1974 Tax Model and TAXSIM.

enough to demonstrate the importance of incorporating endogenous behavior response in revenue predictions. The final column shows the dead-weight loss of the deduction, evaluated according to the procedure given in equation 3. Because all marginal rates are driven toward zero by the change, the dead-weight loss of the change is always negative. The reader may note the relatively high ratio of dead-weight loss to revenue at high income levels, reaching 10 to 1 at the highest level.

Child Care Credit. The child care credit started as a deduction, but was converted to a credit in 1976. The current rule allows 20 percent of dependent care expenses to be taken as a credit against tax due. Expenses are limited by the secondary earner's actual earnings, and by $2,000 for each dependent up to two such dependents. The 1981 law raises the dollar limit to $2,400, but also introduces a sliding scale for the credit which increases the rate by 1 percent for each $2,000 that the taxpayer's income falls short of $30,000, with a maximum rate of 30 percent.

The effect of the child care credit on the wife's marginal after-tax wage rate is quite a bit more complicated and less exactly modeled than the secondary earner's deduction. There are three paths for the credit to affect the after-tax wage. First, the expenses subject to the credit are

TABLE 7

BASE LINE DATA FOR THE CHILD CARE CREDIT, 1979

AGI Class ($)	Number of Returns (1,000s)	Mean AGI ($)	Tax Liability ($)	Child Care Expenses ($)	Wages (secondary earner) ($)
5,000–10,000	47	9,609	80	640	2,316
10,000–15,000	157	12,980	727	550	4,543
20,000–30,000	1,090	25,190	2,984	972	8,715
30,000–50,000	759	36,300	5,469	175	11,090
50,000–100,000	79	62,850	14,540	709	14,750
Greater than 100,000	11	141,700	47,770	805	19,240
Mean		27,616	3,780	707	8,669
Total	2,590	7.15×10^{10}	9.79×10^{9}	1.83×10^{9}	2.24×10^{19}

NOTE: Returns claiming child care credit are included. Returns with AGI less than $5,000 are excluded from table but are included in totals.
SOURCE: U.S. Treasury 1977 Tax Model and TAXSIM.

limited by the amount of earnings for the secondary worker (or $166 per month for a full-time student). Second, changes in earnings will affect AGI, which in turn will affect the percentage credit allowed for individuals with AGI between $10,000 and $30,000. Third, changes in hours worked presumably affect the actual expenditures required for child care. The exact specification of this last relationship is obviously not possible, so we make the simplifying assumption that marginal expenditure on child care equals average expenditure on child care. That is, expenses will be proportional to hours of work supplied. Of the three effects, it is the first that is most affected by the liberalization of the credit.

Although single parents are eligible for the credit, only married couples are included in the simulation, chiefly because little is known about the labor supply response of single men and women.[31] The same wage and income elasticities are used as in the simulation for the secondary earner's deduction, in the absence of evidence to the contrary.[32]

Average child care expenses and secondary earner's wages are given by income class in table 7. The expenses seem small compared with the wages earned, and it would be interesting to know just what these expenses represented.

Table 8 shows the effects of liberalizing the child care credit. For moderate incomes the feedback of the secondary earner's wages into the

58

TABLE 8

EFFECTS OF LIBERALIZING THE CHILD CARE AND DEPENDENT CARE CREDIT, 1979 LEVELS

AGI Class ($)	Tax Liability		Change in Hours Worked	Change in Dead-Weight Loss ($)
	Exogenous behavior ($)	$\eta_w = 0.5$ ($)		
5,000–10,000	−50	−47	−3.5	0.50
10,000–15,000	−47	−49	−3.2	0.54
15,000–20,000	−63	−68	−4.4	0.66
20,000–30,000	−24	−30	−6.5	8.85
30,000–50,000	−4	−4	−0.7	6.97
50,000–100,000	0	0	0	0.4
Greater than 100,000	−20	−24	−1.3	2.35
Mean	−26	−29	−3.9	4.34
Total	6.56×10^7	7.51×10^7	1.02×10^7	1.1×10^7

NOTE: Only those claiming credit are included.
SOURCE: U.S. Treasury Tax Model 1977 and TAXSIM.

credit rate acts to raise the marginal tax rate. This lowers the after-tax wage rate, and when combined with the reduction in tax liability caused by the increased size of the credit, results in a substantial decline in hours worked. Below $10,000, only the income effect is present, but the ten-point increase in the amount of the credit leads to a similar effect. The overall effect is a four-hour reduction in annual work effort. The $29 loss of revenue is accompanied by a $4–5 increase in dead-weight loss. The credit may have been intended to encourage mothers to enter the labor force. Because it is keyed to expenses, however, rather than to earnings, it cannot have that effect. An exception to the rule would be the rare case where child care expenses exceeded earnings, in which case the after-tax wage rate is raised by 20 to 30 percent of the pretax level. This applies to only 2 percent of our sample. Because marginal rates are raised, the dead-weight loss of this tax reduction is positive, a remarkable event, though not without precedent.

Concluding Remarks

The departure from marriage neutrality under the current U.S. income tax system is quite substantial. The average amount of penalty paid by the 18.7 million couples whose tax liability would be lower if they were allowed to file as single individuals is $481, and the corresponding gain for each of the 20.3 million couples who benefit from joint filing is a startling $713. Only 6 percent of couples are not affected.

We have seen that no positive income tax system can achieve the simultaneous goals of marriage neutrality, horizontal equity, and progressivity and that it might be expected that a device such as the secondary earner's deduction might enhance the first goal at the expense of the latter. The success of the SED in reducing the marriage penalty, however, is almost matched by its success in increasing the marriage benefit for those couples who benefit, and by the transfer of many couples from the penalty to bonus categories. The total marriage penalty is reduced from $9.3 to $7.3 billion, while the marriage bonus is increased from $13 to $14.7 billion. The net result is a slight decrease in the average deviation from neutrality.

The SED also leads to a slight increase in labor supply by married women—perhaps fifteen hours per woman per year. The behavioral response has a significant effect on the estimated revenue cost of the deduction, reducing that estimate by about one-third, to $72 per joint return. The reduction in dead-weight loss (relative to a nondistorting distribution of the same reduction in revenue) is about twice the revenue loss. Although popular literature has emphasized the equity argument for a special treatment of secondary earners, we have seen that the deduction can be recommended only for its positive efficiency effect.

A similar examination of the liberalized child care credit leads to the conclusion that it is a tax reduction which lowers after-tax wage rates. The average recepient of the credit gains about $29 in tax reductions but works about four hours less. There is a net increase in dead-weight loss of $4–5.

On narrow efficiency grounds one might be tempted to endorse the secondary earner's credit and condemn the liberalization of the child care credit, but there are quite good reasons to oppose both measures. The tax code has come so far from the simple tax on "income, from whatever source derived" authorized in the Sixteenth Amendment to the U.S. Constitution that a cynical public has come to believe that the definition of taxable income is a purely political matter without any factual basis. Certainly the history of family taxation does little to discourage this notion. As the traditional principles of Haig-Simons income are forgotten, we do not necessarily move toward efficient Ramsey taxation, and each departure from Haig-Simons income, no matter how well justified on efficiency grounds, encourages further departures without as good justification. The resulting system is likely to distort far more the uniform system left so far behind us.

Notes

1. A comprehensive history of the controversy is given in Alicia Munnell, "The Couple versus the Individual under the Federal Personal Income Tax," mimeographed, Federal Reserve Bank of Boston, 1978. Also see June O'Neill's paper in this volume.

2. See Spencer Rich, "Sintax," *Washington Post*, July 26, 1979.

3. Michael J. Boskin and Eytan Sheshinski, "Optimal Tax Treatment of the Family: Married Couples," NBER Working Paper No. 368 (1979). See also Harvey S. Rosen, "What Is Labor Supply and Do Taxes Affect It?" *American Economic Review*, Papers and Proceedings, vol. 70, no. 2 (May 1980), pp. 171–76, and Munnell, "The Couple versus the Individual."

4. Lynda Moerschbraecher, "The Marriage Penalty," *Tax Notes*, March 2, 1981, p. 427. This argument implicitly assumes that a husband's labor supply is not sensitive to tax rate changes generated by his wife's earnings.

5. Peter Mieszkovski and John Shoven have both pointed out that a proportional income tax could be combined with a uniform lump sum capitation grant to each individual. The resulting tax and transfer system could be quite progressive, at least at low- to moderate-income levels, if the lump sum grant was sufficiently generous, and the system would clearly be neutral with respect to marriage. In 1979 aggregate adjusted gross income was $1,464 billion, which yielded revenues of $214 billion. Given the population (220 million) and assuming static behavior, we can use a simple arithmetic identity to yield the marginal tax rate necessary to raise the same revenue. That rate is 0.15 for a lump sum grant of zero, and increases by 0.015 for each $100 of the grant. Although a system of this kind has many attractions, surely marriage neutrality is among the least of them.

6. Because the credit is available to married and single individuals, changes in the child care credit do not strictly affect the marriage tax. It is included here because marriage and children are still intimately related for most Americans.

7. Emil M. Sunley, "Statement before the House Ways and Means Committee on the Tax Treatment of Married and Single Taxpayers," U.S. Treasury, April 1980.

8. See Harvey S. Rosen, "Taxes in a Labor Supply Model with Joint Wage-Hours Determination," *Econometrica*, vol. 44, no. 3 (May 1976), pp. 485–507; R. E. Hall, "Wages, Income and Hours of Work in the U.S. Labor Force," in E. Cain and H. Watts, eds., *Income Maintenance and Labor Supply* (Chicago: Rand McNally, 1973).

9. Daniel Feenberg and Harvey Rosen, "Alternative Tax Treatments of the Family, Simulation Methodology and Results," in M. S. Feldstein, ed., *Simulation Methods in Tax Policy Analysis* (Chicago: University of Chicago Press, 1983).

10. In the section on methodological issues in behavioral simulation, the issue of data imputation is taken more seriously, but the imputation of deductions is a peripheral issue that will be described here. Each couple on

the CPS tape was assigned an amount of deductible expense chosen randomly from those joint returns on the 1977 tax model with the same income and number of children. Returns were grouped in brackets $1,500 wide, and families with more than four children are grouped together.

11. In order to bring all figures to 1979 levels, we increase all dollar amounts by the proportional change in taxable income from 1974 or 1977 to 1979 and increase the number of returns according to population growth.

12. Institute for Social Research, Survey Research Center, *A Panel Study of Income Dynamics; Procedures and Tape Codes 1974 Interviewing Year; Wave VII; A Supplement* (Ann Arbor, Mich.: Institute for Social Research, Survey Research, 1974).

13. It has been used, for example, to create the Brookings MERGE file. See Joseph A. Pechman and Benjamin Okner, *Who Bears the Tax Burden?* (Washington, D.C.: Brookings Institution, 1974).

14. Criteria for doing the matching are discussed by J. B. Kadane, "Some Statistical Problems in Merging Data Files," U.S. Treasury, Office of Tax Analysis, in *1978 Compendium of Tax Research*, 1978, pp. 1201–22, and B. Barr and J. Turner, "A New Linear Programming Approach to Microdata File Merging," in U.S. Treasury, Office of Tax Analysis, *1978 Compendium of Tax Research*, 1978, pp. 131–50.

15. Feenberg and Rosen, "Alternative Tax Treatments of the Family."

16. Hall, "Wages, Income and Hours of Work."

17. James Heckman, "Sample Selection Bias as a Specification Error," in Smith James, ed., *Female Labor Supply* (Princeton, N.J.: Princeton University Press, 1980), pp. 206–48.

18. Jerry A. Hausman, "The Effects of Taxes on Labor Supply," mimeographed, MIT, 1980.

19. For a comprehensive discussion of the theory the reader is referred to James Heckman, Mark Killingsworth, and Thomas McCurdy, "Recent Theoretical and Empirical Studies of Labor Supply: A Partial Survey," mimeographed, University of Chicago, 1979.

20. Hausman, "Effects of Taxes on Labor Supply," analyzes a model with fixed costs of work, and Rosen, "Taxes in a Labor Supply Model," discusses a model in which full- and part-time workers receive different hourly wages.

21. Hall, "Wages, Income and Hours of Work."

22. This includes own- *and* cross-wage effects. For households in which the wife is the primary earner—that is, her earnings exceed her husband's—the wife's labor supply is assumed to be perfectly inelastic.

23. See, for example, Heckman, Killingsworth, and McCurdy, "Recent Studies of Labor Supply," pp. II.28, II.34. Hausman, "Effects of Taxes on Labor Supply," also finds a small wage effect but a fairly substantial income effect.

24. Hausman, "Effects of Taxes on Labor Supply."

25. Clearly, this procedure cannot be implemented for nonworkers. For these individuals the following ad hoc procedure is used: calculate the

average H, w, and A for members of the individual's group who work between zero and 100 hours. Substitute these means into equation system 3 and use the implied values of a, b, and s for nonworkers.

26. See Farrel Block, "The Allocation of Time to Market and Non-market Work," Stanford University, Institute for Mathematical Studies in the Social Sciences, 1973; Rosen, "Taxes in a Labor Supply Model," pp. 485–507.

27. Jerry A. Hausman, "Exact Consumer's Surplus and Dead-weight Loss," *American Economic Review*, vol. 71, no. 4 (September 1981), pp. 662–76.

28. Robert Willig, "Consumer's Surplus without Apology," *American Economic Review*, vol. 66, no. 4 (September 1976), pp. 589–97.

29. See Kenneth Small and Harvey Rosen, "Applied Welfare Economics with Discrete Choice Models, Exact Consumer's Surplus and Dead-weight Loss," *Econometrica*, vol. 49, no. 1 (January 1981), pp. 105–138.

30. Feenberg and Rosen, "Alternative Tax Treatments of the Family."

31. This included 70 percent of returns claiming the credit in 1977.

32. In the simulation for the secondary earner's deduction, inelastic response was assumed for the primary earner, and elastic response only for the female secondary earner. With the 1977 data the sex of taxpayers is unknown, and a few male secondary earners are inevitably given an elastic labor supply response.

Commentary

Bernard Saffran

In order to analyze the effects of the changes in the tax treatment of married couples, Feenberg has presented a paper with two parts that have a similar subject matter but use different methodologies. The first section is a static analysis (that is, it assumes no labor supply response) of the tax implications of marital status and is similar to a number of studies that have appeared on this subject, most recently one done by Emil M. Sunley when he was deputy assistant secretary for tax policy. The second section, using the methodology developed in the earlier Feenberg-Rosen paper, focuses on the effects that the provisions of the new tax law regarding the secondary earner's deduction and the child care credit will have on labor supply, tax revenue, and economic welfare. Both parts of the paper indicate how far the profession has come from back-of-the-envelope discussions of tax questions. The first part does an excellent job of updating the tax policy literature to take account of the recently enacted provisions for the deduction of secondary earner's income. The second part, however, is of more academic interest because it uses many new and sophisticated techniques and is concerned with the labor supply response of married women, who are subject to high marginal rates and have good alternative uses for their time, and so are the demographic group that recent studies have led us to believe should have the largest labor supply response. In both sections of his paper Feenberg has presented us with the state-of-the-arts analysis, but I will argue that in the second section the additional sophistication may not have helped to increase the precision of the results.

To begin, I do have a problem with the iso-revenue iso-penalty lines for those with an income above $50,000, since in the early part of the paper Feenberg indicates that he has no observations at these income levels. The tax code has a large number of provisions that depend on the marital status of the taxpayer, and so, for example, though it is common to refer to *the* marriage tax penalty, there really are a number of such penalties. Some idea of the elasticity of interpretations that

64

can be applied to this concept are found in a recent paper by Peter K. Cook,[1] in which the author cites twenty-one provisions of the tax code that he interprets as imposing some form of marriage penalty (these range from widely cited differences in marginal tax rates, to less well-known rules about the level of unemployment insurance that needs to be included in the tax base, to some fairly obscure provisions dealing with complex business transactions). He makes the strong claim "that 90 percent of married couples can arrange a divorce in such a way that, with proper tax planning, their combined tax liability would decrease after divorce."[2] If we could assume that all taxpayers were this sophisticated about their tax planning, then it would lead to far larger estimates of a marriage tax penalty than have been presented by any other analyst, including Cook. I am in no position to evaluate this claim, but it does point to an important issue—the quantitative estimates of the marriage tax will depend not only on the provisions of the tax code that are considered relevant but also on the assumed sophistication of the taxpayer.

Even if we could assume that all taxpayers were sophisticated and knowledgeable, I recognize that neither Feenberg nor any other analyst has the data that would allow him to make all of the necessary adjustments. I would, however, still like to comment on some of the assumptions that are made in the first part of the paper. First, the paper does not make clear whether Feenberg assumed that "head of household" rates apply if the marriage was terminated and there were children. Later discussion indicates that this was his assumption. Secondly, we need to examine the appropriate treatment of itemized deductions. In the first section of the paper Feenberg assumes that the itemized deductions are related to income and the number of children, but he does not take into account the possibility that divorced couples will have many more opportunities to shift their deductions to minimize their tax liabilities. Sunley's paper does provide us with some estimates of this effect. In a similar static analysis, he finds that there is about a $5 billion (from $8.3 billion to $13 billion) difference in the marriage tax liability if the divorced couple shifts deductions to minimize taxes. Had Feenberg assumed more sophisticated taxpayers, he would have found a much larger estimate of the marriage penalty. It seems to me that the orders of magnitude of these tax management effects are such that for purposes of estimating revenue, it might be more important to focus study on the sophisticated techniques of taxpayers than on the sophisticated techniques of tax analysts.

The last section of the Feenberg paper drops the static labor supply assumptions and provides estimates of the labor supply, revenue, and welfare effects of the introduction of the secondary earner's deduction as well as the changes in the child care credit. To put the methodology of this section into perspective, not too long ago the effects of changing tax rates, credits, and deductions on labor supply would have been studied by assuming either that these changes had no effect on labor supply or that the coefficient of the exogenous pretax wage rate could be used to find the effect of taxes on labor supply. In this paper Feenberg is able to use the whole panoply of techniques that have recently been developed specifically to deal with some of the problems that arise because the budget constraint becomes nonlinear from progressive taxation and possibly even nonconvex because of still other provisions of the tax code. Instead of the ad hoc comments about the welfare implications that have been so common in the tax literature, Feenberg is able to use Jerry Hausman's methods for sharp estimates of excess burden. In this section, Feenberg demonstrates his knowledge of the issues. He knows the road well and is aware of the placement of the potholes.

Although, in principle, I am convinced that the techniques that have been developed to analyze nonproportional taxation have greatly expanded our understanding of the issues and do represent a major technical advance over those used earlier, I am concerned as to whether these techniques ought to be applied to the data that Feenberg uses. The major problem with the data is that it consists of tax returns which only have earnings and some demographic variables, and so in order to use these techniques Feenberg must make a large number of assumptions and impute values for the missing variables. I wonder, however, whether making his set of assumptions leads to better answers than were obtained with the older assumptions either of fixed hours or of treating the wage rate as the appropriate exogenous variable. By removing one known source of bias, Feenberg may be adding some unknown sources of bias as well as some additional variability in the estimates. Most of these issues can be illustrated by examining his derivation of the parameters of the indirect utility function. From equations 1 and 2 it is clear that even if we grant him the form of the function, his estimates require a knowledge of the after-tax wage rate, hours worked, and effective income, as well as the wage and income elasticities.

Feenberg's primary data source for his estimates of wages and hours is a sample of tax returns. These, of course, do not provide information on the taxpayer's wages and hours. To help him to solve this problem, he uses another data set, the University of Michigan Panel Survey of Income Dynamics (PSID), which has data on wages and earnings as well as some demographic variables that are also available on the tax returns. Unlike other analysts who combine the data to form synthetic observations, Feenberg simply uses the wage relationship found in the PSID to impute a wage rate (with a residual added) to the married women in the tax sample. He then uses this rate in combination with earnings data in the tax returns to find annual hours. A related problem is finding the wages and hours for nonmarket workers to use in finding the parameters of their indirect utility function, and here he just operates with some ad hoc procedures. The difficulties of integrating data sets and the correct specification for nonmarket workers are endemic to this sort of research, and until we have surveys that include the necessary tax data and develop better techniques for analyzing nonmarket workers, we will have to expect that, depending on the assumptions that are made, there will be unavoidable variation in the estimates.

Let us return to Feenberg's derivation of the parameters of the indirect utility function. To identify these parameters he must assume that the labor supply function is linear, and he needs estimates of the wage and effective income elasticities. Arguing that previous studies have found that the linear labor supply specification was useful, he then uses a survey by Heckman, Killingsworth, and McCurdy to find his estimates of the elasticities. I have a great deal of trouble with this procedure. The reason for Feenberg's use of techniques that require the parameters of the indirect utility function is that if the nonlinearity and nonconvexities of the budget constraint caused by the tax system are not correctly modeled, we will not have good estimates of the effect of changes in taxes on hours worked. In fact, however, with the exception of the Hausman study, all the studies that are cited in the survey ignore the endogenity problems caused by the tax system (and Hausman's results were not directly applicable, because his sample was only of the low-income black population). I should say that I do not see the point of developing new techniques and then of using values for the crucial parameters that rely on the discarded techniques. I do feel, however, that there is a partial defense for Feenberg's using these values of the elasticities, though it might not be one he would care to take—he could argue that those who are willing to accept the conventional analysis should accept his as well since he just uses the same parameter values in a more general theoretical framework. Even taking this generous view of his procedures, it is difficult to say if the results are "reliable" since, without synthetic cohorts, we cannot tell if the wages and hours that were used were consistent with the observed elasticities. As is made clear in the Feenberg-Rosen paper, many of us have not yet learned to have any intuition about what are "reasonable" results.

Let me suggest a number of partial and imperfect approaches for getting a feel for the reliability of his quantitative results. First, there is Feenberg's comparison of his results when we allow for an endogenous labor supply response. Compared with exogenous labor supply situations, there is an average increase of fifteen hours of work a year and $33 in revenue. Although Feenberg agrees that the labor supply response is "slight," he feels that the revenues effects are "significant." I feel that these results just serve to emphasize the second-order nature of the effect we are examining. At least with the exogenous labor supply assumption we know the direction of the bias of the results, but, as I have mentioned, when we use his more complex procedures for estimating the endogenous labor response, we often do not even have a good intuitive idea of the outcome.

Some additional sense of the importance of the reported effects can come from a comparison of the values in the status quo situation in the Feenberg and Rosen and the Feenberg papers. Before the meeting I asked Feenberg why these numbers differed, and he told me that different samples were chosen and that different stratification procedures were used in the two studies. The average difference between the two status quo effects here is fifty hours a year of work and $847 in taxes. Once again, given the great deal of variability between the status quo values in the two samples, how much is gained by using these procedures? I am not challenging Feenberg's arithmetic, but is seems to me that his answer is not terribly robust, that we are searching for very subtle effects with very imperfect instruments and data, and that if Feenberg had chosen a different sample or a different set of reasonable initial assumptions, he might well have found a very different effect.

Although I have been critical of many of his procedures, I do feel that it is as fine a piece of work as can be done with the available data and techniques. I stand in awe of Feenberg's ability to generate such sophisticated results from such little data. Feenberg has answered the questions put to him using state-of-the-art techniques (and I must also admire the speed with which he has been able to incorporate the new provisions of the tax law into this simulation), but given his combination of assumptions and data, the results in the second part must be viewed as being largely of methodological rather than policy interest.

Notes

1. Peter K. Cook, "The Frustrations of the Marriage Tax," *Tax Notes*, August 10, 1981.
2. Ibid., p. 265.

Peter Mieszkowski

I am more sympathetic than was Bernard Saffran to the latter part of Daniel Feenberg's paper, and I shall restrict my comments to that section. The first part contains the simulations of the marriage penalty, and the second part deals with revenue effects and dead-weight losses. In reading the paper, I have concentrated on trying to interpret table 6. The most important result is that if we cut taxes by means of the secondary earner's deduction, we get about one-third of the tax revenues back in the form of additional labor supply effects.

The reason I find this paper interesting is that it goes against much of my intuition. Maybe my intuition is terrible, but one aspect of my intuition is that I thought that the welfare loss or the dead-weight loss effects would be relatively small. Perhaps I am extrapolating too much from my own family circumstances, but in our case the secondary earner's deduction is really like a lump sum transfer and does not change the marginal tax rate. The numbers reported earlier, however, suggest that in fact the marginal tax rates do go down, and certainly that is what Feenberg has said in the paper. Perhaps there are other aspects of the tax law that lead to a decrease in marginal tax rates.

A more general point is contained in the earlier Feenberg-Rosen paper, where they found a number of things that surprised them. This is progress in the sense that we are finding out things that we did not anticipate. As they pointed out in their paper, it is due to the fact that the tax system is much more complicated than indicated by any one particular dimension that we may be examining. The striking thing, however, is that if I take the dead-weight loss estimates seriously, they are very large indeed. They are large for every income group. The most striking one is for the group with an adjusted gross income of greater than $100,000. There is a decrease in the inefficiency or the dead-weight loss of $606, whereas the revenue loss leads to a ratio of the reduction of the dead-weight loss to the revenue effect of 10 to 1 as Feenberg interprets it. It is simple to see, however, that the relationship between the dead-weight loss and tax revenue associated with the secondary worker's deduction is of the order of 2 to 1.

I remember that when I heard Jerry Hausman's results for the first time, they seemed very large relative to conventional wisdom. I am not sure where the conventional wisdom comes from. It probably comes from Harberger triangles that were calculated in the early 1960s. That approach implied a very small efficiency loss relative to total tax revenue collected. So whatever reservations we may have about the results stemming from Saffran's comments, I think these results are quite important, and one of the issues is whether this magnitude of the dead-weight loss results are specific only in the above $100,000 income class.

This raises a more general question. Even if there is no significant labor force response because of offsetting income and substitution effects, are we going to find estimated welfare losses that, if perhaps not as striking as these, are very significant? We teach, or at least I always teach, that if income/substitution effects wash out so that taxes do not have much effect on labor force response, there is still a dead-weight loss. I confess, however, that I have never really had my heart in the argument until now. Earl Rolph and others in the 1960s suggested that we should have a generous tax credit and then integrate the positive income tax and negative tax by having a marginal tax that is constant over income classes.

Why do I mention this? Given that the taxation of the family unit creates a tension between marriage neutrality, horizontal equity, and progressivity, one can ask, Why not throw out progressivity? I think Feenberg's results support this approach, though I am not absolutely certain, because if we raise the marginal tax rate to a third and keep that constant, it is quite possible that a number of household units are going to be subject to higher marginal tax rates than they are at present. Thus, I find this paper very interesting, though I am a little uneasy because of the magnitude of some of the results.

Discussion Summary

In responding to Bernard Saffran's comments, Daniel Feenberg admitted that there was a problem in developing a complex model of behavior based on utility analysis and then introducing labor supply elasticities based on much less sophisticated studies. In theory the analysis could have been based on much more sophisticated estimates of labor supply responses, but that would have greatly complicated the paper, and Feenberg indicated a desire to keep things simple.

Feenberg did not believe that the large difference in the estimate of base hours worked between this paper and the earlier Feenberg-Rosen study created a serious problem. He was mainly interested in the *change* in hours worked caused by the change in the tax law, and the estimate of that change is not likely to be affected much by a difference in the estimated base.

Feenberg agreed with Peter Mieszkowski that the estimated dead-weight loss was very high. He noted, however, that it was the labor supply of married women that was being discussed. The dead-weight loss associated with income taxation could be expected to be higher because the labor supply of married women is known to respond to taxes more than that of married men.

John Shoven noted that Mieszkowski made an important point in referring to the effects of the progressive rate schedule on the size of the dead-weight loss. Shoven noted that current income tax revenues could be raised with a single marginal rate of 30 percent combined with a generous $1,400 per person tax credit. In such a system, most of the current problems related to the taxation of singles versus married couples would disappear. He also noted that the current degree of progressivity could be attained by combining such a system with a surtax on incomes above $75,000—something that would affect very few people.

Ronald Hoffman suggested that estimates of dead-weight loss may be higher in Feenberg's paper than in earlier analyses by Harberger because Feenberg's data were aggregated much less and, as a general rule, one obtains higher welfare loss estimates with less aggregate data. The aggregation process cancels negative distortions against positive

71

distortions and thus produces a downward bias in the dead-weight loss calculation. Mieszkowski agreed that this is correct.

Gene Brannon asked whether Feenberg's analysis took account of the value of work done in the home. Feenberg replied that the utility-maximizing model did take this into account in that at the margin the value of an additional hour of leisure or work in the home was equated to the after-tax wage. It is through this process that the reservation wage is established.

The Tax Treatment of Households of Different Size

Eugene Steuerle

Perhaps no change in the nation's tax laws has been more significant, yet less recognized, than the shift since the late 1940s in the relative tax burdens of households of different size. For both single and married persons with dependents, the tax burden has grown dramatically relative to households without dependents, whether measured by dollars or by average tax rates. Even the much heralded "marriage penalty" resulted less from an actual shift in relative tax burdens—singles received a tax reduction of only about $420 million in 1971 when income splitting was abandoned—than from the recognition by two-earner couples that they were not receiving the same tax treatment on a per-earner basis as were single individuals and unmarried couples.[1]

This shift in the tax burden of households of different size came about in subtle ways, without, as far as I can determine, any explicit debate by policy makers about the shift or even about whether it was intended. The shift occurred primarily because of a passive public policy toward dependents of taxpayers: personal exemptions were kept relatively constant while incomes of taxpayers increased substantially.

Perhaps one reason for this passivity has been the decline in average household size over recent decades. Certainly the rapid increase in the number of one- and two-person households would make less controversial the increased relative tax burdens of households with three or more members. Another factor may have been the lack of agreement on the proper tax policy regarding dependents. Although numerous theories are espoused, they often produce contradictory results. In examining these various theories, I conclude that there is more than a reasonable basis for granting tax allowances on the basis of household

I am grateful to Harvey Galper, Graham Patterson, Emil Sunley, and Eric Toder for helpful comments and discussions. The views expressed are those of the author and do not reflect Treasury policy.

size and that these allowances are appropriate at all income levels. I tend to prefer exemptions over credits and find partial income splitting to be as justifiable for dependents as for spouses. But those views are less strongly held than my belief that, whatever the type of tax allowance, it should be large enough to compensate adequately for most differences in ability to pay, at least between households with dependents and households without dependents.

Changes in Family Allowances, 1948–1984

The principal means by which the Tax Code adjusts for family size is through the personal exemption. The personal exemption currently is $1,000 and is scheduled to stay at that level until 1985, when it will be indexed for inflation. In 1948, however, the personal exemption was $600. If the personal exemption had been indexed for income growth since 1948—in other words, if the exemption were to offset the same percentage of per capita personal income today as it did in 1948—then it would equal $4,600 in 1981 and rise to about $5,600 in 1984.

By almost any measure, this decline in the personal exemption has been the largest single change in the income tax in the postwar era. Exemptions on taxable returns originally reduced the tax base by about 24 percent of total personal income during each year of the period from 1948 to 1954; today, the reduction is only about 8 percent. Even those numbers understate the magnitude of the decrease because exemptions formerly excepted large portions of personal income for nontaxable households as well.[2] Indeed, the increase in the tax base due to the decline in the personal exemption, and the accompanying decline in adjusted gross income (AGI) of nontaxable individuals, completely offsets the much more widely recognized decline in the tax base from *all* other sources: increases in net exclusions from AGI, itemizations, standard deductions, and credits.[3]

Changes in two other major tax provisions have had much smaller, although significant, effects on the distribution of tax burdens among households of different size. First, tax rate schedules have been altered. Prior to 1948, there was only one rate schedule for married persons, heads of households, and single persons; if both spouses had incomes, however, they could file separate returns. Income splitting was available only in community property states. In 1948, income splitting was made universal for married persons, and in 1969 the rates for singles were lowered, thereby reducing the "single penalty" and increasing the "marriage penalty." For 1982 and thereafter, married couples will be allowed a partial deduction for the earnings of the spouse with lower earnings.

Second, there have been frequent changes in the zero bracket amount (ZBA) or standard deduction. Currently, the ZBA differs between joint returns on the one hand and the returns of singles and heads of households on the other. Like the tax rate schedules, there has never been an adjustment in the maximum amount of standard deduction or ZBA according to the number of dependents, whether cared for by married persons or single persons as heads of households. Thus, whenever family size adjustments are made through the ZBA, they tend to allow no reduction in tax liability for dependents.[4]

Although the standard deduction or ZBA was increased many times, especially in the 1970s, it offsets only a slightly larger portion of personal income than it did in the early 1950s. Standard deductions on taxable returns equaled about 4.5 percent of personal income during each year of the period, 1947 to 1953, fell to about 2.6 percent by 1963, rose to a maximum of 7.3 percent in 1977, fell again to about 5.4 percent by 1981, and under current law will fall continually relative to income after 1981, although at a reduced rate after indexing is introduced in 1985.

Tables 1 and 2 demonstrate the net result of changes in exemptions, tax rates, and ZBAs (or standard deductions) on the tax burdens of households of different household size. Table 1 compares taxes for households with incomes equal to median family income, assuming that a constant percent of income represents itemizable expenses. During the period from 1948 to 1981, and extrapolating to 1984, the tax burden of singles grows at a slightly lower rate than the tax burdens of joint returns with no dependents. As a percent of total income, however, the increase in tax burden for both is just under 5 percent. For house- holds with dependents the change is much more dramatic. For joint returns and heads of households with two to four dependents, the increase over the same period ranges between 8.3 percent and 10.1 per- cent of income. Indeed, in 1948 most of these households paid no tax at all.

These changes in relative tax burdens are persistent throughout the whole period, 1948–1984. For instance, single persons and married couples with no dependents are scheduled to face essentially the same average tax rates in 1984 as they did in 1960. For households with dependents, however, average rates rise dramatically over the same period. A couple with two dependents has an increase of about 43 per- cent (from 6.9 percent to 9.9 percent) in its average tax rate, while for a couple with four dependents the increase equals 223 percent (from 2.6 percent to 8.4 percent).

In table 1 it is assumed that all households have incomes equal to median family income and that they itemize their deductions. A similar

75

TABLE 1

Taxes for Households with Median Family Income, by Filing Status and Number of Dependents, 1948–1984

| | | Single | | Joint | | | | | | Head of Household | | | |
| | Median Family Income[a] | | | 0 dependents | | 2 dependents | | 4 dependents | | 2 dependents | | 4 dependents | |
Year	($)	Tax ($)	Tax as percentage of income	Tax ($)	Tax as percentage of income	Tax ($)	Tax as percentage of income	Tax ($)	Tax as percentage of income	Tax ($)	Tax as percentage of income	Tax ($)	Tax as percentage of income
1948	3,187	300	9.7	208	6.5	9	0.3	0	0.0	109	3.4	0	0.0
1954	4,167	534	12.8	402	9.6	162	3.9	0	0.0	282	6.8	42	1.0
1960	5,620	780	13.9	625	11.1	385	6.9	145	2.6	511	9.1	265	4.7
1966	7,532	962	12.8	741	9.8	524	7.0	328	4.4	668	8.9	451	6.0
1972	11,116	1,544	13.9	1,201	10.8	916	8.2	631	5.7	1,108	10.0	814	7.3
1978	17,640	2,602	14.8	2,101	11.9	1,768	10.0	1,408	8.0	2,093	11.9	1,722	9.8
1981[b]	24,400	4,154	17.0	3,229	13.2	2,755	11.3	2,281	9.3	3,238	13.3	2,724	11.2
1984[b]	29,600	4,293	14.5	3,375	11.4	2,935	9.9	2,496	8.4	3,468	11.7	2,988	10.1

NOTE: This example compares taxes for different size households earning the same income for various years between 1948 and 1984. Median family income was chosen in order to hold constant the relative status of the households being compared over those years. At income levels both above and below the median, there are similar trends in changes in taxes for households with dependents relative to households without dependents. The example assumes itemizable expenses equal to 23 percent of AGI in all years. For 1984, no allowance is made for a deduction if the married couple has two earners.

a. Note that the median family income does not represent the median income of the household units of various sizes. Singles have lower income than families, partly because the population of singles is concentrated in among the young and the aged. Families with dependents have higher incomes than all families because workers in families with dependents are usually in their prime working years.

b. For 1981 and 1984, median family income is projected by taking median family income for 1979 and increasing that income by U.S. government projections of changes in the consumer price index. Tax/income for 1981 and 1984 change little when rates of income growth are projected through different methods.

SOURCE: Median family income—U.S. Bureau of the Census, *Money Income of Households, Families and Persons in the United States.*

TABLE 2
TAX-EXEMPT LEVELS OF INCOME BY FILING STATUS AND NUMBER OF DEPENDENTS, 1948–1984

			Joint			Head of Household	
Year	Per Capita Personal Income[a] ($)	Single ($)	0 dependents ($)	2 dependents ($)	4 dependents ($)	2 dependents ($)	4 dependents ($)
1948	1,425	667	1,333	2,667	4,000	2,000	3,333
1954	1,783	667	1,333	2,667	4,000	2,000	3,333
1960	2,226	667	1,333	2,667	4,000	2,000	3,333
1966	2,992	900	1,600	3,000	4,400	2,300	3,700
1972	4,555	2,050	2,800	4,300	5,800	3,550	5,050
1978	7,871	3,200	5,200	7,200	9,200	5,200	7,200
1981	10,900	3,300	5,400	7,400	9,400	5,300	7,300
1984	13,208	3,300	5,400	7,400	9,400	5,300	7,300
Percentage change 1948–1984	+827	+395	+305	+177	+135	+165	+119

a. For consistency, per capita personal income for 1981 and 1984 were projected to increase at the same rate as median income in table 1.

SOURCE: For per capita personal income—U.S. Bureau of Economic Analysis, *The National Income and Product Accounts of the United States; Survey of Current Business.*

shift in relative tax burdens shows up at other income levels as well. Table 2 shows the shifts by household size in the minimum levels of income for which taxpayers owe any tax liability at all. These tax-exempt levels of income are determined by the standard deduction or ZBA and the personal exemption.[5]

Although the ZBA in the near future will reduce the tax base by about the same percent of personal income as at the beginning of the 1950s, its general use in setting tax-exempt levels of income is partly responsible for the shift in tax burdens among households of different size. Tax-exempt levels of income for families of four have been kept just about at the official poverty level throughout most of the postwar period.[6]

In the Revenue Act of 1964, Congress explicitly acknowledged the intention of establishing a tax-free level of income approximating the poverty level. The method it adopted at that time and since then, however, was to increase the minimum standard deduction, but not the personal exemption.[7] Increases in the amounts of standard deduction are the same for couples with and without dependents, while increases in exemption levels are worth more to couples with dependents. Thus, tax-exempt levels for households without dependents have been moving closer and closer to tax-exempt levels for households with dependents.

Another influence on the relative tax burden of families of different size, at least from 1964 to the late 1970s, was the way in which the official poverty level was adjusted from year to year. Official poverty levels are redetermined each year by multiplying the previous year's poverty level by the percentage change in the consumer price index (CPI) between the two years. Incomes, however, have increased faster than prices. As long as Congress connects the use of the exemption and standard deduction to a price-indexed poverty level, their combined importance must continue to decline relative to income. When the dependency exemption declines relative to income, as noted before, the tax burdens of larger households move closer to those of smaller households.

There are several reasons why the standard deduction was favored over the exemption. Increasing the standard deduction was a cheaper means of raising tax-exempt levels; such increases were of no benefit to taxpayers who continued to itemize. Moreover, increases in the standard deduction supposedly simplified the Tax Code by limiting the number of those who itemize. Finally, since exemptions for taxpayers and dependents were linked to exemptions for the aged, Congress may have been reluctant to increase tax-exempt levels for the aged at a time when their tax-exempt income from social security was increasing rapidly.

Whatever the public policy intent, tax-exempt levels of income rose much more slowly than income for all household sizes. For a family of four, for instance, the tax-exempt level in 1954 was about one and one-half times per capita personal income in the economy (see table 2). For 1981 the situation is reversed, and per capita personal income is about one and one-half times the tax-exempt level of income. Single persons had increases in tax-exempt levels greater than those that applied to joint returns with no dependents, but the difference was not nearly as great as between returns without dependents and those with dependents. Joint returns with no dependents, for instance, have increases in tax-exempt levels of 305 percent between 1948 and 1984; for joint returns with two dependents, the corresponding number is only 177 percent. For joint returns with more than two dependents, and for heads of households with dependents, the increases are even smaller.

These changes in tax-exempt levels, of course, refer only to income subject to taxation. As noted above, increases in exclusions for certain types of income have partially offset the decline in the exemption. In particular, income-conditioned transfers and social security income usually are excludable from taxation. Since most social security income is received by households without dependents, its exclusion also tends to favor smaller households relative to larger ones. On the other hand, food stamps and aid to families with dependent children are conditioned upon size of household. For households receiving these transfers, the effective tax-exempt level for economic income will vary with size of household more than on the basis of adjusted gross income. Nonetheless, most households receiving income-conditioned transfers have economic income (AGI plus excludable income) which does not exceed tax-exempt levels.[8]

Theories of Equity and Incentives

There are a number of theories and considerations that influence tax policy regarding households of different size. Although there is some overlap, I have combined these considerations into two groups. The first group involves theories of equity which fall broadly into one of two categories: family assistance and ability to pay. Related closely to the theory of ability to pay are issues that are often ignored, yet may be implicit in the choice of type and size of tax allowance. These issues include the taxation of transfers, the investment or consumption nature of expenditures for dependents, and, finally, comparisons of intertemporal tax burdens over the life cycle. The second group of theories deals with incentive questions: the effect of taxes on the supply of work, on savings and investment, on population growth, and on the amount of dependent care provided. This group will be treated in a later section.

These theories or considerations often produce reasonable but conflicting results. I have therefore attempted, while reflecting my own preferences, to present this material in a comprehensive framework that will relate and balance these conflicting considerations.

Family Assistance. According to this theory, an allowance for dependents is designed to ensure some minimum level of well-being for each dependent. The theory generally extends beyond taxpayers to non-taxpayers as well, and the minimum level of well-being is implicitly set by the maximum cash grant or tax credit available per child. The theory calls for a credit or grant based on family size, although the allowance may phase out as income rises.[9] If a tax credit is provided by the tax system, while a grant is used in the welfare system, the two systems may not mesh well, especially for those households that are in both systems

79

at the same time. A common goal of welfare reform effort is to bring the two systems together in some logical fashion, such as replacing the personal exemption with a per capita credit integrated through both the welfare and tax systems.

While the use of a credit is perhaps most appropriate under a family assistance theory, at various times substitution of a personal credit for the personal exemption has been proposed as a means to increase the progressivity of the tax system. It is often asserted that a credit is more progressive because the value of the exemption increases as marginal tax rates increase. In general, this argument is fallacious. Given any family size, exemption level, and rate structure, it is possible to design a credit and alternative rate structure that will give exactly the same level of progression.[10] Thus, the choice between a credit and an exemption, except under the constraint of a fixed rate structure, is not one of progression at all. It is primarily a question of how, at any given pretax income level, adjustments for tax liability should vary according to family size. Credits, for instance, will grant equal relief for each additional dependent. Exemptions will grant lesser relief as the number of dependents increase and the taxpayer moves to lower marginal rate brackets.[11]

Ability to Pay. The traditional ability-to-pay argument assumes that families are the appropriate unit of taxation. If ability is to be measured by income, but only after some adjustment is made for subsistence costs, however defined, then the tax base will equal income over and above these subsistence costs.[12] As noted above, this was essentially the theory that was followed in setting exemptions and standard deductions from the mid-1960s through the late 1970s. Official poverty level budgets were equated with subsistence levels, and positive tax rates began at income levels above poverty levels, at least for smaller families.

The poverty level budget attempts to measure "equivalent" standards of living for different size families. By taking into account economies of scale, externalities of consumption, or the "public" or "club" nature of goods used by the household, it is determined that the incremental amount of income necessary to support an additional household member generally declines as household size increases.[13]

The Tax Code, however, adopts an "equivalency scale" only at tax-exempt levels of income. At higher standards of living, a comparable equivalency scale would require greater absolute income differentials for similar increases in household size. For instance, suppose that a couple is living at the poverty level, and $1,000 of additional income would be required to maintain a poverty level of consumption if a dependent is added to the family. Then the standard of living available to a couple living at the poverty level and a couple with a child is exactly the same if the latter has $1,000 more income than the former. If, however, other families generally provide their dependents with more than poverty levels of consumption, then a $1,000 exemption is inadequate to adjust for family size at most levels of income. Such considerations led A. C. Pigou to argue that dependent deductions should increase with income.[14]

Let us refine the rule under which horizontal equity is applied to the tax system under the ability-to-pay principle. It is sometimes stated that those with equal incomes, after adjustment for household size, should pay equal tax. This is somewhat misleading. At its root, ability to pay calls for equal sacrifice (total, as well as marginal) among equals, not equal tax. A better statement of the rule would be as follows: *households with equal before-tax ability to maintain a standard of living should have an equal after-tax ability.*

An example will demonstrate how this rule can be applied to the issue of taxation according to size of household. Suppose that a family of three needs an income level equal to 125 percent of the income of a family of two in order to have an equal ability to maintain the same standard of living. If a family of two has $20,000 of before-tax income, and a family of three has $25,000, the rule does not imply that both families should pay the same amount of tax. On the contrary, if the family of two pays $4,000 in taxes, then the family of three needs to pay $5,000 in taxes in order that both families have after-tax incomes which allow them to maintain the same standard of living.

This logic strongly supports the case for income splitting among household members. If there are economies of scale in the household, however, each household member should not be granted the same exemption level, zero bracket amount, and other bracket widths. Instead, a type of income averaging is called for.[15] For instance, in the above example, a third family member would be attributed one-fifth of total family income, but that additional one-fifth would be taxed at the same average rate as applied to the remaining four-fifths of family income (the remaining four-fifths would be taxed as if it were earned by the two-person family).

Three observations are appropriate here. First, an equivalency scale, if it could be derived, may not require the same degree of income splitting at all income levels. At very high income levels, for instance, the addition of a family member may require a much smaller additional fraction of income to support the same standard of living. Vickrey, for instance, argues that "the presumption that dependents share in the family resources in some proportion to needs becomes weaker as the income increases."[16] Second, the issue of income splitting is not one of progression; any degree of progression can be reached by adjusting the rate schedule. The question is whether those with before-tax incomes sufficient to maintain equal standards of living should have after-tax incomes sufficient to maintain equal standards. Without splitting, households with dependents would have lower after-tax abilities even though they had before-tax abilities equal to those of households without dependents.[17] Third, this principle can be applied equally well to a progressive consumption tax as to a progressive income tax. An income tax taxes the ability to maintain a given standard of living, while a consumption tax taxes the standard of living itself. Nonetheless, the notion of income equivalency is not too different from a notion of consumption equivalency, and splitting would be equally applicable to both types of taxes.

If there are economies of scale, the ability-to-pay argument may also be used to justify smaller allowances or exemptions as household size increases. On equity grounds, smaller allowances would be required if smaller increments of income are needed to maintain a given standard of living as family size increases. From an efficiency standpoint, however, the argument can be stood on its head and used to justify increasing allowances as family size increases. Economies of scale imply that many consumption goods used within the household are in the nature of "public" or "club" goods for the household public, or, more narrowly, goods for which there are positive externalities within a close physical environment. Since more persons may share in the consumption of a good in a larger household, aggregate consumption may actually be increased by making transfers from smaller families to larger families. If one accepts the notion of an income equivalency scale such as in the poverty budget, then less income per person is needed to provide a given level of consumption in larger families. Yaakov Kondor argues that transfers to larger families are especially appropriate even when there is already equality in the sense of equal "income per equivalent adult" of each family (that is, when families of different sizes are considered equally well off after adjusting for family size, composition, etc.).[18] For the same cost, more people can enjoy the good being consumed, and thus welfare may be increased.

Related Theories and Considerations. Three issues are closely related to the theory of ability to pay.

The taxation of transfers. One difficulty in applying ability-to-pay arguments to tax treatment of households is that income is transferred to dependents. There are a few areas of tax law on which there is less agreement than transfers.

If income is perceived only as rewards to factors of production, then transfers are not income to recipients. In arguing against income splitting for spouses, for instance, Moerschbaecher states that "the Internal Revenue Code is premised on the taxation of the entity earning the income, and that the concept of sharing of income . . . is simply not the theory on which our entire income tax system is based."[19] On the other hand, if income is to be taxed to the person "enjoying" or consuming the income, then it is the transferee, not the transferor, who should be taxed. Michael McIntyre and Oliver Oldman, for instance, argue that family income spent or saved by the parents for the benefit of their children is properly taxable to the children.[20] In any case, if transfers are taxed to recipients, while donors are taxed on income which is transferred, then some income would appear to be taxed twice. If both a donor and a recipient have the ability to use income as they wish, however, then both have an increased ability to pay resulting from the transferred "income"—after all, over time both could have consumed the income if they wished.

Current law is ambiguous as to which of these views is correct and has adopted no consistent treatment of transfers. Income is generally taxed to the earner because administratively it is difficult to measure who consumes the income. Tax brackets for joint returns, however, are widened relative to single returns, thus allowing some couples to treat a portion of the income as being transferred between them. In the case of alimony, payments are deductible to the transferor but taxable to the recipient. Child support payments, however, are viewed as similar to obligations of parents living with their children and, thus, neither taxable to the children nor deductible to the transferor. In the case of large transfers of wealth, some of the transfers may be taxable under the estate and gift tax, even though the income generating the transfer may first have been taxed under the income tax.[21]

When transfers are deemed to be charitable, they receive especially favorable treatment; if the donor itemizes deductions, the income generating the transfer is taxable neither to the donor nor the recipient. Various special rules attempt to prevent "personal" transfers from being deductible; for instance, one can give deductible contributions to the poor through a legally exempt organization but not directly. Although deductions are allowed only for certain "social" purposes, the distinction between eligible and ineligible organizations seems to be based not so much on need—a visitor to a museum, a college student, or a member of a church is probably no more needy than the average person—as on the remoteness of the transferor from the transferee. From an administrative viewpoint, this makes sense, as it is almost impossible to monitor personal transfers. The limitation is also attributable, I believe, to a perception that incentives for giving are not necessary for persons close to us or for small groups with closed membership. Incentives, however, are needed to generate giving to persons remote from us and to large organizations which offer their services freely to all.[22]

There is no easy resolution of this debate. One general rule seems to be that transfers are deductible to the transferor if those transfers are for purposes desired or expected by society, for example, charitable transfers, transfers to spouses, and some amount of transfers to dependents. Still, the code is not consistent in its treatment of transfers. Complicating the issue further is that in the case of intrafamily transfers, it is generally impossible to know the exact amount of income transferred, so that, even if the transferee is to be taxed, one must resort to devices such as exemptions and income splitting as approximations. Moreover, capital income and some self-employment income is already easily redistributed among family members so as to minimize tax burdens, while wage and salary income cannot be redistributed at all; thus, more than complete income splitting is available for capital income,[23] while no splitting at all is allowed for wage income. Finally, personal exemptions can be taken by children against their own income at the same time that the parents claim dependency exemptions. This double exemption violates all theories of the taxation of transfers.[24]

Dependents as consumption and investment. Related closely to the question of transfers is the correct labeling of the services provided to dependents, in particular, children. Do these services indicate consumption by the providers, consumption by the dependents, or investment in the dependents? Although I recognize the extreme limitations of applying such economic labels to activities that are often better analyzed and understood from a social perspective, the tax treatment of any transaction is dependent upon the economic label given it, so the label may as well be accurate.

The trend in recent years toward equalization of tax burdens regardless of number of dependents implicitly reflects the view that the raising of children is primarily a consumption good to the providers. Typical of this belief is the statement by Henry Simons, "It would be hard to maintain that the raising of children is not a form of consumption on the part of parents."[25] Accordingly, parents should be granted no tax relief for a type of consumption that they choose to enjoy. Related to this view is the premise that the services of a homemaker are provided primarily to the homemaker or to the homemaker's spouse, rather than to dependents such as children. Thus, many authors regard as inequitable the nontaxation of goods provided in the home.

If, however, most of the services are not provided to the homemaker, but represent income or consumption of the dependents, then we should be less bothered if the provider of the services is not taxed on the recipient's income. Moreover, if the recipient's total income is less than some reasonable tax-exempt level of income, then nontaxation of both homemaker and dependent may indeed be an appropriate solution. As for actual cash outlays for the recipient, they also should be taxed at the marginal rate relevant to his standard of living rather than at the higher marginal rate that would apply if such expenditures were treated as consumption of the providers. Thus, income splitting would be appropriate for such expenditures.

In the case of children, many of the services provided by the care-taker and the goods transferred by the original earner of the income may not even be consumption. A society which uses such phrases as "investment in our youth" is one which believes, rightly or wrongly, that many expenditures of money and time on dependents are investment, not consumption.

The Tax Code treats investment in physical assets as eligible for investment credits. Moreover, future flows of cash from investment are not all taxed; through capital cost recovery or depreciation allowances, the entire investment can be recovered without taxation (indeed, some have argued that capital cost recovery provisions yield an effective rate of taxation of income from depreciable assets that may be negative).

In the case of investment in human capital, the tax treatment is different again. Many educational goods and services are provided free to individuals. The income devoted to that investment is deducted by the charitable giver, the property taxpayer, and indirectly by the student and parent who "pay" for these services through forgone earnings.[26] By the same token, the value of the investment is not "recovered" over the life of the investment. Cash wages of an individual are not only a return on human capital, but also a depreciation of the capital. There-fore, the deduction of the cost of educational services may compensate for the nondepreciation of the human capital (indeed, it is equivalent to expensing of the investment). In the case of educational services pro-vided through cash payments from private, noncharitable sources, how-ever, no deduction is allowed for the expense, and no depreciation is taken over the life of the recipient.

If the care of children is investment in human capital, neutrality as well as equity would argue for tax treatment similar to that provided for other investments. Obviously, since there are different treatments of different types of investment, several comparisons could be made. Under any comparison, it would not be unreasonable to allow some deduction for the expense of investment in both cash outlays and the forgone earnings of caretakers. To the extent that the investment results in a later increase in the wage income of the dependent, the deduction is especially warranted because, as noted above, no depreciation is allowed against future wage receipts even though those receipts include a return of capital as well as income from the capital.[27]

One can carry this argument to an extreme. As Harold Groves states, were one to argue that "consumption outlays . . . are a cost of maintaining the labor supply, one could easily stretch this doctrine to exclude all income from the tax base."[28] A balanced position, it seems to me, would be that some portion of the services and goods provided to children, especially those which are educational, could reasonably be classified as investment and therefore deductible.

The life-cycle distribution of tax burdens. Many persons view the choice of tax allowances for dependents only on the basis of within-period differences in ability to pay between households with and without dependents. There is a danger, however, in comparing the tax burdens of different households at only one point in time rather than over a life cycle. The proper treatment of dependents is as much a question of the intertemporal distribution of tax burdens for each person as one of the distribution among persons in households of different size. At one point in our lives practically all of us are dependents in a household, and at other points in our lives most of us care for dependent children or parents. Even if all of us came from households of equal size and had an equal number of dependents, we still might want a tax system that takes account of differences in ability to pay according to periods in which we belonged to households with dependent children. Disregarding problems of transition to a new tax system for taxpayers who have already lived a good part of their lives under a given tax system, the choice of tax allowances for dependents is in large part a decision as to the distribution over time of our own lifetime tax burdens.

Incentive Theories

Incentives to Work, Save, and Invest. From the standpoint of incentives to work, save, and invest, the tax allowance for dependents with the greatest incentive effect would be to allow some form of income splitting. Increases in personal exemptions and credits reduce the tax base by setting aside a certain amount of income to be taxed at a zero rate. Under a fixed revenue constraint, providing tax allowances for dependents by increasing dependency exemptions or credits results in an increase in the average rate of tax on the remaining tax base and may therefore result in an increase in average marginal rates as well.[29]

This argument can be carried only so far. As long as other changes may be made in the tax laws, increased exemptions and credits can also be used in connection with policies that favor lower average marginal rates. For instance, the rate schedule that applies to the taxable base itself can be made more proportional. Dependency exemptions can also be separated from other personal exemptions. It should also be noted that an exemption provides a greater lowering of average marginal tax rates in the population than does a reduction of the lowest rates in a progressive rate schedule. The latter change is equivalent to a flat credit for all persons with marginal rates above the lowest rates, while exemptions lower taxable income and therefore reduce the marginal tax rate of some persons at all income levels.

Population Policy. According to one theory, any adjustment for family size lowers the tax burden of the family and is therefore an incentive to have children. Mirrlees "suppose[s] that most orthodox economists would take this view, that excessive population makes the environment unpleasant, and that parents should choose family size under the constraint of paying for these external diseconomies."[30]

While I find extreme the view that the marginal value to society of any child (or any adult, for that matter) is negative, there seems to me to be little justification in tying tax allowances for dependents to a population policy, no matter what the goals of that policy. The tax system is not well designed for population measures. In truth, the system can affect the actual decision to have children only by punishing or rewarding the caring for dependents after they are born. Zero or low allowances for child dependents would likely imply low allowances for elderly and disabled dependents as well.

Actually, tax allowances for children, even if fully adjusted for ability to pay, would still be a fairly small percentage of income. For instance, a dependency exemption of $1,000 increases the after-tax income of a median income family by only about 1.1 percent in 1981. Changes in these tax allowances are therefore likely to have only small effects on the net cost of raising children. Much more significant in affecting the net cost of raising children have been other institutional changes, such as the development of reliable public and private retirement systems. In some societies, children are expected to support parents in their old age; this makes the net *individual* cost of bearing children much lower than in a society where the children provide such support through public rather than private support, or parents provide for their own retirement.

Finally, it should be noted that if tax allowances for dependents do have strong incentive effects, and if the cost of caring for dependents is considered to increase with income (for example, higher income individuals would provide more education and housing to their offspring), then almost any design of dependent allowance other than partial income splitting is likely to create perverse effects across income classes by offsetting the cost of childbearing and care of elderly parents more for one class than another. A similar observation regarding differences between welfare allowances and tax allowances has been made by Gerard Brannon and Elliott Morss.[31]

Incentives for Caring for Dependents. Dependents are by nature individuals who must rely on others for some or most of their care. Society as a whole recognizes an obligation to care for these individuals, although it accomplishes this care primarily through the family. In cases in which the family cannot provide, alternative sources of income are made available either through welfare or social security. In starkest terms, societal programs today are based primarily upon the assumption that care of dependents is inelastic with respect to both price and income (at least at incomes above welfare levels). Thus, not only are tax allowances for dependents limited, but family assistance payments are available only for dependents in poor families, and charitable transfers usually are deductible only when made to remote or large groups.

If society instead were to care for all dependents through government programs, the revenue cost—and related efficiency cost—would be staggering. Relying on the family is therefore a fundamentally sound and efficient approach. Nonetheless, I think it would be a mistake to pass over this issue without at least noting that if there is some elasticity of response to caring for dependents, then there may be indirect costs to keeping the tax allowance low.

As I argued regarding population policy, however, almost any tax allowance is likely to make only a small differential in the cost of caring for dependents or not caring for them,[32] and its direct incentive or disincentive effect is therefore likely to be small. Perhaps of more importance here may be the symbolism involved. If families with dependents lower their standards of living more through payment of taxes than do families without dependents, then the former group may indirectly come to believe that society places little value on dependent care. More likely, however, societal values influence the tax policy rather than flow from it.

Summary and Recommendations

Since World War II, the tax burden of households with dependents has grown dramatically relative to households without dependents, whether for single or married categories. One reason for this shift in tax burdens has been the lack of any consistent agreement on the proper tax policy regarding dependents.

My review of the theories and considerations regarding tax allowances for dependents has led me to believe that these allowances are appropriate and that the current dependency exemption is inadequate by almost any standard. Tax allowances are unnecessary only if income should be taxable to the original earner, regardless of the standard of living the earner can obtain, if investment in dependents or expenditures for their consumption are to be treated as only consumption of the donor, or if the Tax Code is a relevant and useful tool for implementing an accepted population policy of discouraging childbirth. Each of these requirements is in my opinion unacceptable or unmet, though not irrational.

If the view of the tax allowance is that it is only meant to provide family assistance at low income levels, then the current allowance may be adequate or even unnecessary at higher income levels. This view should also find the current exemption to be rather awkwardly designed: the amount of assistance at low income levels is quite small, and the assistance is much more related to the needs of the taxpayer alone (through zero bracket amounts and taxpayer exemptions) than to additional needs caused by dependents (through dependent exemptions).

Ability to pay, however, is the standard equity theory by which the tax system is normally judged. If ability is to be measured by income above subsistence, then the current exemption is inadequate according to the existing "official" measure of poverty or subsistence. While this measure and other measures of poverty and subsistence are subjective and may be criticized for a variety of reasons, they have tended over the last two or three decades to rise only with the price level and, therefore, to decline relative to income. At the same time, the exemption for dependents has remained relatively constant and has not even increased with the price level.

The theory of ability to pay holds that units with equal ability should make equal sacrifice. The notion of income equivalency recognizes that a large household will not be able to maintain the same standard of living as a small household with equal income, but that the difference is not proportional to the number of individuals in each household. The setting of tax-exempt levels of income higher for larger households, but not proportional to the number of family members, means that income equivalency, however subjective may be its measurement, is inherent in the structure of the tax system. Then to deny the same tenet at higher income levels is inconsistent. As a result, the current Tax Code violates the principle that those with equal ability to maintain a standard of living before tax have an equal ability after tax.

If transfers are treated as income to the recipients, or if the care of children involves some component of investment as well as consumption, then tax allowances for dependents are again appropriate at all income levels. A tax allowance similar to income splitting would again be called for, although the rate of splitting could reasonably be thought to decline at higher income levels. If transfers are taxable to the transferee, some notion of an equivalency scale still seems to be necessary to avoid full income splitting among all household members.

If taxes for each person are to be adjusted for life-cycle differences in ability to pay according to periods in which the person resides in a household with dependents, then tax allowances for dependents are a reasonable means of making such an adjustment. And finally, if one is concerned with the symbolism behind tax measures, and if society places a value on both dependent care and work outside the home, then a neutral signal—one that acknowledges the inherent value of both types of effort—might be a dependents' allowance. The allowance better recognizes the extent to which household care—at least the level of care that society expects—reduces the standard of living that can be maintained by the taxpayer.

How might we move from here to there? My own compromise proposal would be to allow, for joint returns with dependents, the use of a tax rate schedule in which brackets are at least twice as wide as those that apply to single persons. Such income splitting would eliminate the marriage penalty for couples with dependents and, in addition, recognize that the ability to pay of a family with dependents is lessened by the presence of dependents.

Another rate schedule would be provided for heads of households with dependents and to married couples without dependents. This schedule might be estimated from the single schedules by assuming some income splitting, such as 70:30. Heads of households would pay lower taxes relative to singles than they do now; those without dependents and filing joint returns would pay a greater share.

The change for heads of households would be especially significant. They have had the greatest increase in taxes (relative to singles and those filing joint returns) over the previous three decades; moreover, as long as the marriage penalty is reduced outside of the rate structure, their tax burden relative to the tax burden of those filing jointly will continue to increase.

Any remaining marriage penalty could be addressed with a device (even optional filing), which would be much less complicated than all current options simply because there would be a smaller percentage of couples with any potential marriage penalty. The addition of a third schedule also makes explicit that income splitting is being allowed for dependents and would logically, therefore, be accompanied by a requirement that dependents' income be pooled with the family's income for tax purposes.

Similarly, I would provide that there be three ZBAs: one for single returns, a second for joint returns with no dependents and returns of heads of households, and a third for joint returns with dependents. The ZBA for joint returns with dependents would again be at least twice as large as for single returns. Since the ZBA is the first bracket in the tax tables, this change can be accomplished simply by applying the same splitting formula to both the positive and zero rate brackets.

Finally, the dependency exemption would be separated from other personal exemptions and raised from its current level at approximately the rate of growth of per capita income. This solves the problem of introducing too many rate schedules and at the same time makes some allowance for larger family sizes. Those attentive to questions of population or marginal tax rates may be somewhat concerned with the raising of the exemption level. Much of the additional tax allowance for dependents is granted, however, by lowering rates through the addition of only one rate schedule to apply to all households with one or more dependents; the concern therefore should be minimal.

My principal conclusion is that adjusting for family size is reasonable at all income levels and should compensate for differences in ability to pay between households with dependents and households without dependents. Such changes can be made under almost any requirement of tax progressivity and with little or no effect on various incentives or disincentives that might be desired. Finally, whatever policy that is adopted should be made explicit; changes in the relative distribution of tax burdens across family size should be made by conscious choice and not as the accidental outcome of passive public policy.

APPENDIX TABLE 1

THEORIES OF TAX ALLOWANCES FOR DEPENDENTS

	Supportive of Tax Allowances for Dependents	*Adequacy of Current Tax Allowances*	*Further Remarks*
		Equity Theory	
Family assistance	Yes	Inadequate at low income levels (if the tax system is meant to provide this assistance)	The current tax provides only a small amount of assistance at low income levels; welfare programs have usually been used to provide family assistance.
Ability to pay			
Equal tax for taxpayers with equal levels of income above subsistence payments	Yes	Inadequate at "poverty" levels, especially for larger families	Equivalency scales are implied at subsistence levels, but not at other income levels.
Related or supporting theories			
Tax transferor	No	—	Some exception is usually made for transfers necessary to provide a subsistence-level standard of living for the family.
Expenditures on dependents as consumption of taxpayers	No	—	Again, an exception is usually made for subsistence-level income, implying that only expenditures on dependents above subsistence levels are consumption to taxpayers.

Equal sacrifice for equals (equal after-tax ability to maintain a standard of living for those with equal before-tax ability)	Yes	Inadequate at all income levels	Partial income splitting is required with progressive rate structure. Similar arguments would apply under a standard of living measure of equity with a consumption tax.
Related or supporting theories			
Tax transferee	Yes	Inadequate at all income levels	Limits are usually placed on extent to which transfers are added to recipients' income but subtracted from donors' income. Examples: gifts to friends, large wealth transfers. Perhaps only transfers "desired" by society should be deductible to donor, e.g., charitable gifts, care of dependents.
Expenditures on dependents as consumption of dependents	Yes	Inadequate at all income levels	Without resorting to equivalency scales to measure ability to pay of transferee, dependent's portion of family income will be taxed under tax rate schedule similar to taxpayer's.
Lifetime considerations (vary taxes over life cycle)	Yes	Inconclusive	Size of allowance depends upon extent to which taxpayers wish to take account of ability to pay *between* periods according to presence of dependents.

(continues on next page)

APPENDIX TABLE 1 (continued)

Incentives Theory

	Supportive of Tax Allowances for Dependents	Adequacy of Current Tax Allowances	Further Remarks
Work, savings, and investment	Indifferent	—	Related design of overall tax structure may be important; income splitting gives greatest decline in average marginal rates, *ceteris paribus*.
Population	No (if disincentives desired) Yes (if incentives desired)	—	Even if disincentives or incentives are desired, the tax system may be an inappropriate vehicle; incentive levels are probably too low to make much difference.
Care of dependents	Yes	Inconclusive	Incentives probably make little difference; if symbolism is important, one measure of neutrality may be to require equal sacrifice for equals.
Investment in human capital (or expenditures on dependents as investments)	Yes	Inconclusive	Size of allowance depends partly upon extent to which other investments are expensed; consideration may be based more on equity across investments than efficiency since no incentive is provided if amount of investment is assumed in setting allowance.

SOURCE: Author.

Notes

1. The revenue cost of allowing married couples the option of being taxed as singles is much greater than the revenue gain from reducing the single rate schedule so as to provide for income splitting.

2. Nontaxable households include those who filed, but owed no tax, and those who did not file.

3. Michael Hartzmark and Eugene Steuerle, "Individual Income Taxation, 1947–79," *National Tax Journal*, June 1981, pp. 145–66.

4. There are some exceptions. Between 1964 and 1970, there was a minimum standard deduction which increased by $100 per dependent for taxpayers meeting certain requirements.

5. During the years 1975–1978 a general tax credit also increased the tax-exempt level of income. The general tax credit was replaced after 1978 with an increase in the exemption level.

6. Generally, Congress has compared poverty levels and tax-exempt levels only for singles and for families of four, but not for families of size greater than four. Tax-exempt levels have been constantly below official poverty levels for large households.

7. In 1964 singles were judged to have poverty levels which were much higher than one-half the level for a couple; the remedy applied until the late 1970s was to increase the standard deduction for single returns at a much faster rate than for joint returns.

8. Unfortunately, tax and transfer systems are not well integrated in the United States. It is not clear whether transfer income should be taxed through the income tax if that income effectively is being taxed (through a phase-out of the welfare benefit) within the transfer system. By the same token, it is not clear whether the tax-exempt level should be defined by the income level at which the transfer income begins to phase out, or the level at which taxes paid exceed transfers received.

9. Howard W. Hallman, "A Proposal for a Graduated Family" Center for Governmental Studies, Washington, D.C., 1971.

10. Gerard Brannon and Elliott R. Morss, "The Tax Allowance for Dependents: Deductions versus Credits," *National Tax Journal*, December 1973; Emil Sunley, "The Choice between Deductions and Credits," *National Tax Journal*, September 1977.

11. Although a switch from an exemption to a credit can be designed to provide no change in tax burdens or progressivity among families of a given size, at other family sizes there is a shift in tax burdens. For instance, the design of an equivalent credit structure is usually such that at high incomes, large families would prefer the exemption, while small families would prefer the credit.

12. Alfred Marshall, *Principles of Economics* (London: Macmillan & Co., 1938), p. 135.

13. Note, however, that official poverty levels may show that larger increments of income are needed for typical families as the number of

dependents increases. This is a result of the older average age of children in families as the number of children increases.

14. A. C. Pigou, *A Study in Public Finance* (London: Macmillan & Co., 1928), pp. 101–3.

15. William Vickrey, *Agenda for Progressive Taxation* (Clifton, N.J.: Augustus M. Kelley, 1972), pp. 295–96.

16. Ibid., p. 296.

17. In the simple case where expenditures on consumption equals income, of course, households with dependents would also have lower standards of living.

18. Yaakov Kondor, "Optimal Deviations from Horizontal Equity: The Case of Family Size," *Public Finance/Finance Publiques*, vol. 30, no. 2 (1975), pp. 216–21.

19. Lynda Sands Moerschbaecher, "The Marriage Penalty and the Divorce Bonus: A Comparative Examination of the Current Legislative Tax Proposals," *The Review of Taxation of Individuals* (Spring 1981).

20. Advocating in theory a type of income splitting on the basis of family size, they eventually turn to the exemption (although perhaps varying by number of dependents) as an alternative means of achieving this income splitting. Michael J. McIntyre and Oliver Oldman, "Taxation of the Family in a Comprehensive and Simplified Income Tax," *Harvard Law Review*, vol. 90 (June 1977), pp. 1573–1630.

21. Eugene Steuerle, "Equity and the Taxation of Wealth Transfers," *Tax Notes*, September 1980, pp. 459–64.

22. Richard Goode, in *The Individual Income Tax* (Washington, D.C.: The Brookings Institution, 1976), argues that incentives are the primary purpose of the charitable deduction.

23. Exemptions are available twice for dependents with capital income. In addition, more than a proportional share of capital income may be given to dependents as long as labor income keeps the marginal tax rate of the taxpayer above that of a dependent.

24. One solution to this last problem is to combine together the income of all family members and then to provide tax allowances for dependents, whether they be credits, exemptions, income splitting, etc.

25. Henry Simons, *Personal Income Taxation* (Chicago: University of Chicago Press, 1938), p. 140.

26. See Michael J. Boskin ("Notes on the Tax Treatment of Human Capital," in Conference on Tax Research, 1975, Washington, D.C., 1976) for the argument that the bulk of educational investment is financed out of forgone earnings of students.

27. Note that while this is roughly equivalent to "expensing," it still may imply a positive tax rate if the deduction (e.g., through forgone earnings) is taken at a lower marginal tax rate than the rate which applies to the future flows of wage receipts.

28. Harold M. Groves, *Federal Tax Treatment of the Family* (Washington, D.C.: The Brookings Institution, 1963), p. 10.

29. While *replacing* credits with exemptions, or vice versa, can be designed so that no change is made in overall progressivity, *increasing* either of them under a fixed revenue constraint inevitably means that tax rates on the remaining tax base will have to be increased.

30. James A. Mirrlees, "Population Policy and the Taxation of Family Size," *Journal of Public Economics,* vol. 1 (1972), p. 170. The belief that exemptions influence child-bearing decisions has been reflected in a few bills in Congress. For instance, Senator Packwood once proposed that exemptions not be available for more than two dependent children in any household. See S. 3632, introduced March 25, 1970, and S. 3502, introduced February 24, 1970.

31. Brannon and Morss, "Tax Allowance for Dependents," p. 607.

32. No distinction is made here between indirect costs of caring (forgone earnings) and direct costs (payments for child care). The tax system, partly through the existing credit for child and dependent care expenses, does provide some differential incentive in the method of care provided. That subject, however, is not treated in this paper.

Commentary

Michael J. McIntyre

A reason why Eugene Steuerle and I agree on most of the issues in his fine paper, is perhaps because he and I approach the problems of family taxation from the same starting point. We both agree that the individual income sources of a family member provide an extremely unreliable index of that individual's taxable capacity because of the likelihood that the individual is pooling income sources with other family members. We also agree that a fair system of family taxation should impose tax burdens in accordance with the real changes in economic circumstances that typically, though not invariably, accompany family communal living. Finally, we agree that a family taxation system employing an income-splitting mechanism is best suited to achieve that fairness goal. The only real difference in our positions may be in our understanding of the theoretical underpinning that supports our common starting point.

I reach our common starting point quite directly. As I have elaborated in great detail elsewhere,[1] I believe that the proper taxpayer on income sources earned by one family member and enjoyed by another is the person whose material well-being is augmented by those income sources. That person, in my opinion, is the one who enjoys the consumption and savings that the income sources finance. To implement this benefit principle, I would seek to design a system of family taxation that imposes burdens on family members according to the best available estimates of their share of family revenues. For marital partners, this assumes at least initially that each spouse enjoys one-half the total marital income; for children and other dependents, it assumes something less than a full per capita sharing of the total family income. Combining these assumptions with the benefit principle, I conclude that our basic system of family taxation should permit full income splitting for married couples and should grant much larger dependency deductions for children than we have under current law.[2] Steuerle's data on the diminishing value of the dependency deductions demonstrates how our tax system has become increasingly unfair to parents according to my experience over the past forty years.

The Equal Sacrifice Doctrine

Steuerle reaches quite similar policy recommendations somewhat less directly. He begins by attempting to infuse some content into the old saw that individuals with equal ability to pay should bear equal tax burdens. That old saw, in Steuerle's view, is merely a crude formulation of the equal sacrifice doctrine that economists often employ to justify their version of an ideal income tax.[3] He formulates that saw to say that "households with equal before-tax ability to maintain a standard of living should have an equal after-tax ability."

To draw any policy recommendations from his equal sacrifice principle, Steuerle must first answer a key question: How do we identify those households with equal before-tax ability to maintain a standard of living? Although he does not answer this question explicitly, he does so implicitly through his endorsement of income splitting. What Steuerle seems to be saying is that households have equal ability to maintain a standard of living if the household members have equal per capita shares of the total family income sources, with the caveat that "total family income sources" perhaps should be adjusted for the so-called economies of scale of communal living. Leaving the caveat aside, that is an accurate reformulation of my benefit principle in the traditional equal sacrifice language so familiar to economists.

The following example, adopted from Steuerle's paper, illustrates the compatability of his approach and mine. Consider two families, one with a parent and one child, the other with a parent and two children. Assume that somehow Steuerle has determined that "a family of three needs an income level equal to 125 percent of the income of a family of two in order to have an equal ability to maintain the same standard of living." As Steuerle shows, if the family of two has $20,000 of before-tax income and the family of three enjoys the same standard of living with an income of $25,000, then an equal sacrifice rule would extract $5,000 from the family of three if a tax of $4,000 were imposed on the family of two. This result would be achieved through a variety of mechanisms, one of which would be a flat-rate tax of 20 percent on both families.

The same result could be achieved under the benefit principle by making explicit assumptions, consistent with Steuerle's implicit assumptions, about how income is split among members of a one-parent family. Let us assume that in one-parent families the parent enjoys three parts of the family income and the children enjoy one part each. In a family of two with total income sources of $20,000, the parent would enjoy the benefits of $15,000 and the child would enjoy the benefits of $5,000. For three person families with income sources of $25,000, the parent would enjoy income of $15,000 and each child would enjoy income of $5,000. In effect, therefore, the three-member family would be composed of a two-member family with income sources of $20,000, plus a child with income of $5,000. A flat-rate tax of 20 percent on the income attributed by formula to each family member would result in the family of two paying $4,000 in taxes and the family of three paying $5,000—the result Steuerle achieves under his system.[4]

This example bypasses the complex policy issues introduced by a tax system committed to a progressive rate structure. A per capita income-splitting system presumably would apply to family members the same progressive rate structure applicable to unattached individuals with the same taxable income. I have proposed something less than full per capita splitting, however, because I am unwilling to give children the full benefits of the zero bracket amount (ZBA) of current law, on the ground that the ZBA reflects the welfare needs of unattached individuals, not the needs of dependent children living with their parents. Because of my departure from full per capita splitting for children, I run into problems similar to those that Steuerle faces in determining the relative standard of living of families of different sizes.

Economies of Scale

Steuerle does not endorse full income splitting for married couples without children on theoretical grounds, although he sees some practical advantages of such a system. He proposes a system of partial splitting in order to take account of the benefits of economies of scale which married couples typically enjoy and which frequently are not available to unattached individuals. He would also consider economies of scale in determining the level of dependency deductions. The economies of scale issue should have little or no bearing on the basic issue of income splitting, but it has important enough policy implications that it is worth discussing at least in general terms.

I have trouble with the notion that economies of scale should be considered in designing a system of family taxation, since I believe it opens a Pandora's Box of problems that no tax system can successfully cope with. Economies of scale benefits seem to me to be a special case of what might be called "consumer surplus." I am uncomfortable using the terminology in front of a group of distinguished economists, since I am never exactly sure how economists use that term. But whether or not the term economies of scale falls within the technical definition of economic surplus, it is very much like economic surplus. I see no compelling reason for expanding our concept of income to take into account economies of scale in the family context unless we also are prepared to tax individuals generally on the analogous benefits of consumer surplus. And I am confident that we all agree that adding consumer surplus to the tax base is neither desirable nor practicable.

A couple of examples might clarify my concern. I understand that a fellow who buys cantaloupe on sale at the grocery store is better off economically than someone who pays full price at a roadside stand. I also understand that some people can get great pleasure from chewing a single stick of gum, while others need to chew a whole pack, or take a vacation in Tahiti, to get an equivalent high. But I see no serious way for a tax system to take into account bargain purchases or idiosyncratic responses to market goods and services, nor do I believe that the taxpaying public would want burdens to be distributed according to such nonmarket criteria. And if we are going to ignore nonmarket benefits generally, why do we want to make family cost-saving arrangements an exception to the general pattern?

Perhaps the real reason for the popularity of the economies-of-scale argument is politics. Many individuals view the income tax as an excise tax on income sources and thus perceive income splitting to be some kind of tax preference for married couples. The economies-of-scale argument may be nothing more than an ad hoc response to the political reality fostered by that perception, for it provides an apparently principled basis for mitigating the alleged preference that income splitting provides for most married couples.

Intrafamily Gifts

One of the nice things about Steuerle's equal sacrifice approach is that it neatly sidesteps the issue of intrafamily gifts. My benefit approach, properly understood, also sidesteps that issue, but most commentators do not see it that way, and Steuerle is no exception. Under the benefit approach, income is taxed to the person who consumes or saves the income sources controlled by the family unit. I would approximate that result by ignoring all real gifts and taxing each family member on his or her imputed share of the family income sources. As Steuerle correctly notes, this is functionally equivalent to exempting the donor on income sources shared (actually or imputedly) with other family members and taxing the donee on the actual or imputed gift. Many commentators reject that approach out of hand. They contend that an ideal income tax based on Haig/Simons principles must tax gifts both to the donor and the donee. Stated in Haig/Simons terminology, these commentators believe that income sources spent by parents for the benefit of their children is consumption both to the parent and the child. Steuerle treats this position with more deference than I think it deserves.

Those who favor a double tax on gifts argue that gift giving results in consumption (or savings) both to the donor and the donee. The donee's consumption is obvious, since the donee consumes the market goods and services purchased with the donated income sources. The donor's consumption, however, is of another type, what we might call the delight of gift giving. This delight is classified as consumption in order to explain, in economic terms, why parents decide to give gifts to their children. Arguing backwards from the observed fact of a gift, we can see that an economically motivated parent must have obtained an economic benefit at least equal in value to the market value of the gift or he would not have chosen to make the gift. The logic is impeccable but absolutely irrelevant to the definition of taxable income.[5] A perhaps overly cute example illustrates this point.

Let us suppose that I go home today feeling warm thoughts for my wife, who went to the museum this morning and missed the fine hospitality and lively debate we have been enjoying here. Let us also assume that these warm thoughts lead me to make a gift to my wife of $2,000. Since I choose to make the gift, I must anticipate a benefit in return of at least $2,000—let us say that the delight of gift giving gives me pleasure worth $3,000.[6] If this fable ended here, we would see the classic illustration of the rationale for a double tax on gifts. But let us continue our story. Let us assume that my wife, seeing my absolute bliss from making the gift and wanting the same for herself, gives the $2,000 back to me, also getting a benefit of $3,000. Knowing a good thing when I see it, I give the money back to her, and she to me and I to her, and so forth. In less than an hour we have generated a trillion dollars in taxable income according to the light of the double tax on gifts enthusiasts, and all budget deficit problems are solved.

The fallacy of course is that "income" defined for purposes of studying choice is not always a good index of material well-being. To understand the economic component of choice in nonmarket situations, economists are forced to frame a very broad income definition that takes into account all kinds of imputed and nonmarket benefits which people might care about in making decisions. For example, in understanding why a rich person would marry and share resources with an impecunious spouse, it might be useful to quantify the anticipated nonmarket benefits obtainable from the marital relationship, including the benefits of being married to a physically attractive individual. But that rationale for a very broad definition of economic income provides no basis for making the length of a spouse's nose part of an individual's tax burden calculation. The case for taxing some forms of nonmarket benefits should turn on tax policy considerations, not on a parochial attachment to an income definition drawn from the economics or accounting disciplines.

Going back to my gift-giving fable, let me note one other flaw in the thinking of those who would impose a double tax on gifts. A primary purpose of any tax is to raise revenue for the government. Because almost all taxes raise revenue, however, that purpose provides no basis in most cases for favoring one type of tax over another. But in my gift fable, it is obvious that the government could collect little or no revenue by taxing my wife and me on our gains from gift giving, since neither of us has or could raise the half-trillion dollars we would owe in tax. To collect any tax, the government would have to accept payment in kind—that is, to permit us to pay, literally, with a smile. But as almost everybody knows, a government cannot run on smiles alone.

Notes

1. See Michael J. McIntyre and Oliver Oldman, "Taxation of the Family in a Comprehensive and Simplified Income Tax," *Harvard Law Review,* vol. 90 (1977), p. 1573; McIntyre, "Individual Filing in the Personal Income Tax: Prolegomena to Future Discussion," *North Carolina Law Review,* vol. 58 (1980), p. 469. For a discussion of the benefit principle by an advocate of individual filing, see Gann, "Abandoning Marital Status as a Factor in Allocating Income Tax Burdens," *Texas Law Review,* vol. 59 (1980), p. 1.

2. One nice side effect of income splitting is the elimination of the politically pernicious marriage penalties of current law. For discussion, see Michael J. McIntyre and Robert McIntyre, "The Tax on Marriage," *People & Taxes,* May 1980.

3. For my reservations on the use of equal sacrifice doctrines in tax policy formulation, see Michael J. McIntyre, "Book Review," *Wayne Law Review,* vol. 26 (1980), p. 1181.

4. Steuerle has picked his example chiefly to show the need for dependency deductions under equal sacrifice doctrines. It is too simplified to show all of the relationships between an income-splitting system and a family unit system based on equal sacrifice theories. For a more complex example, see McIntyre and Oldman, "Taxation of the Family," pp. 1602–7.

5. According to wealth tax criteria, some form of double tax on gifts might be acceptable. For example, both the donor and the donee might very well be taxed under an estate and gift tax on property passing from generation to generation. See Eugene Steuerle, "Equity and the Taxation of Wealth Transfers," *Tax Notes,* September 8, 1980, pp. 459, 460–62.

6. My brother, Robert McIntyre, asks, "If pleasure is taxable, is pain deductible?" Or should we assume that anticipated pain is always pleasurable, on the grounds that otherwise it would not have been chosen?

Gerard Brannon

It is unfortunate that Eugene Steuerle began his excellent history with the late 1940s. He is too young to have been through the real war. I have lived through it. Also, my dependents have all grown up and gone away. These are things that affect my viewpoint.

The story before 1948 is interesting, and I think it sheds a somewhat different light on Steuerle's history. In the income tax system of the late 1930s, the allowance for a dependent was only 40 percent of the allowance for a single taxpayer and 32 percent of the per person allowance for a couple. The introduction of per capita exemptions in 1944 was intended as a simplification device and was thought to be too generous to dependents. It did amount to an increase in a dependent's allowance over what it had been, at the same time that individuals and married persons were being cut back. We thought at the time that the introduction of withholding and extending the income tax to a much lower income bracket required some sort of simplification. It is not surprising, then, that this generosity to dependents was later eroded as we were trying to feel our way to something more reasonable. Of course, this whole analysis of how things have changed in a particular year of the past does not say very much. Steuerle recognizes that and gets into a discussion of what the theory of these allowances for dependents ought to be. His approach is first to identify a number of theoretical ways of looking at this question and then to explore each one in some detail. One never knows whether or not his next specific consideration is going to lead one to say the allowance for dependents ought to be more generous or less generous. It is only at the end that he begins to pull things together and his own preferences are seen more clearly.

My remarks are arranged on a little different basis—starting with the end results. I agree with Steuerle that at slightly over the poverty level of income there should be a deduction for each dependent approximating the differential in poverty income for size of family. The concept of poverty income is ambiguous, but Steuerle does not get into specific numbers here and we do not have to argue about that. We both agree that the allowance should, at a minimum, be structured as a deduction that would then rise in tax value with the marginal tax rate—that is, it should not be a tax credit.

These two points of agreement imply that we both reject the extreme version of Henry Simon's view of children as consumption, which would imply no tax allowance whatever for dependents. I disagree, however, with Steuerle's preference for increasing the value of the tax allowance for dependents at high incomes by introducing further income splitting. To support his preference for increasing the differential by family size this way, Steuerle brings in an ability-to-pay argument. We can isolate the issue by assuming that we start with a progressive income tax and assuming that the tax system generates a reasonable (we are not really debating whether it is reasonable) level of tax—say, $30,000 for a childless couple with $100,000. How should this tax change when the couple adds a dependent? The deductions for dependents argument implies that when this couple was childless, the couple had about $95,000 in above-poverty income. In the old days we called this supernumerary income. When one child is added, the above-poverty income declines from $95,000 to $94,000. Roughly, I assume that the differential in poverty income is about $1,000. The present law takes this approach; the differential in the tax for having this one child should simply be this $1,000 difference in above-poverty income. Steuerle's version is that it is not enough for the couple with a child to pay tax on $1,000 less income. He feels there should be further recognition that the marginal utility of income to this family is now higher because there is less above-poverty income per capita. That amounts to about $31,000 of above-poverty income per capita instead of $47,000. According to the usual marginal utility argument, this family with the child should now pay significantly less tax because they are considerably lower on the marginal utility curve.

I am inclined to confront Steuerle's argument with a variant of the Simon position of children as consumption. I went along at an earlier stage in rejecting an extreme version of Mr. Simon's argument that one should make no allowance for children at all because society does recognize an obligation to provide a poverty level of income for any child after birth. This is essentially the commitment that we make in our welfare laws. It follows that if the parent can support the child, we should impose no tax on the amount of income that the parent uses to support the child at the poverty level. Steuerle and I view differently the decision of a family to divide their luxury expenditures, essentially their above-poverty income, with children. Regarding the family with essentially $94,000 of above-poverty income, I do not think it is society's particular concern to change the tax treatment of that income because the family decides to divide it among more people or fewer people. That seems to be the proper business of the family, though I do not go as far as Henry Simon and say that this basic commitment to the child should itself be recognized as pure consumption.

Steuerle buttresses his argument by showing that some of the above-poverty spending on children is investment income, or simply investment, and should be treated more generously in the tax law. Yet the investment in children is already heavily subsidized through government, through the provision of public education. I therefore have difficulty

105

with the tax neutrality toward this subsidized investment. Pursuing this line of thought leads one to think that there ought to be a special tax consideration for families not taking advantage of this publicly subsidized investment in their children, but Steuerle does not pursue that aspect. Finally, in view of the prior discussion we have had about excess burden and dead-weight loss, I am inclined to accept Steuerle's argument that these differentials in treatment of dependents probably have no appreciable economic effect. It strikes me that Mr. Feenberg applied his highly sophisticated demand-curve and utility-curve analysis on this. His analysis probably would show economic effects. It is quite likely that these effects are not equal to zero and also are not very important. After all, an allowance at the $1,000 level must be a small consideration in the whole decision about family size. One would think these tax differentials would be larger and might very well have the kind of effects that could be picked up in a careful analysis.

One of the countries that has previously used the tax technique of income splitting with children is France. As I recall the history, this occurred at a point in time when France perceived itself as having a seriously stagnant population. It was thought that a more generous tax treatment of children would, at least potentially, have some sort of effect in increasing the population rate.

Discussion Summary

Eugene Steuerle agreed with Michael J. McIntyre that it is very difficult to establish an equivalency scale for different sizes of families, but noted that it is done implicitly when computing the poverty line and when establishing an exemption or credit system based upon family size. Steuerle also noted that the McIntyre suggestion of taxing the transferee would require different rate schedules for different people in the family. He felt that it is appropriate to apply notions of economies of scale to the family while not applying them to other groups in society. It is principally in the family that we justify taxing income, through exemptions and rate schedules, to the transferee and not the transferor; therefore, rather than allowing full income splitting for all family members, we are obliged to figure out to what extent these transfers affect ability to pay.

Regarding Brannon's point that a different picture would emerge if Steuerle had compared present-day treatment of dependents with the less generous treatment they received before World War II, Steuerle agreed; his main point, he said, however, was that enormous changes had occurred since World War II that were adverse to large families and that these changes had received little public debate.

Steuerle again emphasized that the issue of how income should be split among family members had little to do with how progressive the tax structure should be. The degree of progression is determined by the tax rate structure. A member of the audience noted that this may be true in theory, but in practice, advocates of different treatment for dependents do not always advocate changes in the rate structure also. Consequently, changes are likely to affect both horizontal and vertical equity.

The panel then discussed whether it is appropriate to subsidize children. Gerard Brannon suggested that it is first important to establish what is fair. That accomplished, discussion could turn toward whether, as a matter of social policy, large families should be encouraged by additional tax exemptions or credits.

Bert Seidman argued that the discussion should focus more on the welfare of children. He suggested that a child brought up in a family with four children should have the same chance as a child brought up in a family with the same income but with only three children. Steuerle replied that the tax system should be made more neutral with respect to having children, regardless of whether society went further in the direction Seidman suggested. Seidman's suggestion would require an extra credit or cash grant in addition to a deduction; at the extreme, government would equalize all costs of raising children—a tenable task up to low levels of income, but too expensive if applied at all income levels.

Bruce Davie asked Steuerle how he would handle the income of dependents. It is now profitable to allocate investment income to dependents since they face lower marginal rates. Steuerle replied that if an income-splitting approach was adopted, the dependents' income should be included in total family income.

Estate Gift Duty and the Family: Prolegomena to a Theory of the Family Unit

Geoffrey Brennan

Introduction

Originally, this paper was to examine the question of how, if at all, family relationships should influence tax liabilities in relation to estates. For the most part, I have been faithful to that purpose. The reader should be warned at the outset, however, that this paper has a tail, and in one sense it is the tail that wags the dog. The considerations that are relevant in dealing with the central question have implications for much broader matters. Specifically, the question of family status in relation to the estate tax is one aspect of the larger question of how family status should be considered when calculating tax liabilities more generally. It is therefore impossible to answer the former question without providing, implicitly at least, the central elements of a theory of the appropriate "tax unit." Therefore, part of my objective here has been to sketch a general theory of the family unit, using the standard approach of orthodox tax theory and using a theory of the family as a social organization that is, in my view, more satisfactory than the newly emergent "household as firm" model.

The tendency toward generalization will come as no surprise to the public finance specialist. It has long been recognized in orthodox tax theory—and particularly since Robert Murray Haig and Henry Simons—that what is normatively relevant is the tax system *as a whole,* and not any particular tax. Therefore, what is horizontally equitable and efficient in relation to estate duties naturally reflects what is horizontally equitable and efficient in the tax system more broadly, and,

NOTE: I am grateful to Michael Brooks and John Head for discussion of much of this material over the past several years.

indeed cannot be satisfactorily determined in isolation from tax arrangements elsewhere in the system.[1] The orthodox thrust toward the *comprehensive* tax system, involving a single progressive tax (or alternatively, a totally integrated set of taxes), is the most familiar application of this general principle.[2]

In relation to the tax treatment of estates, for example, it is widely argued, following Simons,[3] that the *conceptually ideal* arrangement would involve taxing all bequests as income to the recipient/heir (appropriately averaged over the taxpayer's lifetime) on the ground that such receipts add to the recipient's consumption possibilities in much the same way as other forms of income do. The pure Simons approach has, in fact, never been tried in any tax system.[4] It remains, however, a sort of benchmark against which various administrative compromises can be assessed. Certain fairly modest variants have been attempted.[5]

In any case, it seems clear that if the Simons position—and that of orthodox tax theorists who follow him—is accepted, the question of how bequests should be treated within the family will simply be caught up as one aspect of the question of the family under the income tax more generally.

The question of the appropriate tax treatment of bequests impinges on the family unit issue in another way. As Simons clearly recognized, bequests ought properly to be understood in the same terms as gifts or "gratuitous receipts."[6] This is, of course, implicit in the various estate/gift integration proposals. It is equally clear that most private interpersonal giving occurs within the family. I shall argue that the presence of such intrafamily giving represents the prime justification for taking account of family status in determining an individual's proper *total* tax liability. If this is accepted, then whether the integration of bequests/gifts into the personal income tax is considered ideal or not, and whether it is practiced or not, the arguments that surround the tax treatment of bequests are precisely the arguments that bear on the relevance of family status in determining income tax liabilities. I shall attempt to apply these arguments in both contexts. As I have indicated, however, I shall focus *initially* on the estate duty question and on the family unit issue later.

Setting the Stage

The discussion of estate duties that follows presupposes the validity of two central propositions that I shall describe but not adequately defend.

The first is that the "proper" tax treatment of estates is to be viewed in terms of the effect of the tax system *as a whole*. That is, the objective in taxing estates is the two-fold one of imposing on individuals with identical aggregate taxable capacity the same tax burden (the horizontal equity objective) and of minimizing the "excess burden" involved in raising the required (and exogenously determined) level of revenue. It will be recognized here that I am simply following the conventional approach of orthodox tax analysis, as laid out by Haig, Simons, and their more modern expositors. This approach has two important implications for the taxation of bequests:

• A dollar's increase in aggregate consumption possibilities attributable to a bequest received is, in principle, no different from a dollar's increase in aggregate consumption possibilities from any other source. Therefore, I abstract from any additional policy objective, such as the breaking up of large estates for its own sake, which the estate duty might be used for.

• Even if an individual's *wealth* is regarded as an ingredient in determining his proper total tax liability (in addition to his income, however precisely defined),[7] no truly satisfactory case for an estate duty as a "tax on wealth, once a generation" can be advanced: there is simply *no* persuasive horizontal equity or efficiency argument for the estate tax as a surrogate wealth tax. There may of course be *administrative* or *compliance* arguments for using the estate duty in lieu of a wealth tax, but I am ill-equipped to deal with them and, like most public finance theorists, tend to distrust them heartily.

The second general proposition that is relevant here has already been mentioned. It is that all bequests are properly to be treated as acts of *lifetime giving*. This is, in fact no more than a specific application of the general premise of rational behavior on the part of all individuals, since alternative explanations of bequests seem to require some form of irrationality on the testator's part.[8] This view of bequest is essentially that which Simons took.

Given these two propositions, the question of the proper tax treatment of estates reduces to one of the proper tax treatment of gifts more generally—or what Simons referred to as "gratuitous receipts"—with gifts *at the point of death* being simply a subclass.

The major questions here, then, are these: Is there a case for taxing gifts as such at all? Are intrafamily gifts in any way different from gifts of other types?

I attempt to answer these two questions sequentially. In the next section, I set out a formal model of giving, using what seems to me to be the simplest and most logical formulation of the giving relationship. Within this formal model, I deal with tax arrangements explicitly and attempt to show what tax arrangements horizontal equity and efficiency criteria would require.

In the section on alternative models of giving and their tax implications, I distinguish between two other models of giving and briefly indicate the tax arrangements implied by each. The association of intrafamily giving *specifically* with one of the three models enables us to offer an answer to the question as to whether intrafamily gifts ought to be treated differently from other types of gifts. The relevant ends of the argument are drawn together in the section on estate duties and family status. Then in a final section, I attempt to draw the analysis together in a rather different way, focusing on the more general tax unit question.

The Taxation of Gifts and Bequests

Here I develop a theory of the "conceptually ideal" tax treatment of bequests (and gifts *inter vivos*) by examining the effects of alternative tax regimes on the total consumption possibilities of the relevant parties —donor and recipient—within the context of a formal model of interpersonal income transfer.[9] The model can focus initially simply on those two parties, and ignore other taxpayers. Accordingly, let the donor be ascribed a utility function of the form $U_D = F(C_D, C_R)$, where C_D is the donor's lifetime income for own consumption and C_R is the recipient's lifetime consumption (including gifts received). Simply put, this formulation implies that the donor *cares* about the recipient, and that it is this intrinsic concern for the recipient's well-being that induces the donor to make transfers. This model of interpersonal giving seems to be the simplest and most natural. It is certainly familiar in the economics literature.[10]

The recipient is ascribed a utility function of the form $U_R = g(C_R)$. That is, he has no (economically relevant) interest in the donor's well-being. The possibility of reciprocal caring is of course more likely, but we abstract from it in the interests of analytic simplicity.

In keeping with standard public finance analysis, the procedure to be followed in isolating the appropriate tax treatment of gifts involves several steps:

• Isolate the pretax positions of the two parties.
• Determine the tax regime needed to leave pretax relative prices undistorted by taxes (the efficiency requirement, predicated as usual on the assumption that the pretax allocation of private goods is "perfect").
• Determine the tax liabilities that would need to be imposed on the two parties in order to treat them identically with other individuals in the same pretax positions (the horizontal equity requirement).[11]

We consider the efficiency and horizontal equity in sequence.

112

The Efficiency Dimension. We note immediately that there is only one tax regime that leaves the relative price to D of C_D and C_R unchanged. This regime is that in which the donor is taxed on his entire income, irrespective of the use to which it is put, and the recipient is *tax exempt* on all gifts received.[12] In the pretax regime, the cost to D of an additional dollar of consumption by R is one dollar of D's own-consumption forgone. If gifts are taxed when they accrue *both* as income to the donor *and* as income to the recipient, then a dollar's worth of own-consumption forgone by D buys only $(1-t_R)$ dollars of consumption by R. There is, therefore, in this model an efficiency case *against any* taxation of gifts (or bequests)—of either the Simons type or the estate/gift duty type. Gifts and bequests received should be tax exempt in the hands of recipients on efficiency grounds.

The Horizontal Equity Dimension. Would such a policy violate horizontal equity requirements? In fact, the horizontal equity issue is rather complex in this setting and needs to be spelled out in some detail. Consider the diagrammatic depiction in figure 1. The initial pretax, pretransfer equilibrium is at A and involves a level of income to D of C_D^0 to R. The pretax *post*-transfer equilibrium is at E, with a consumption combination (C_D^1, C_R^1): individual D has transferred an amount $(C_D^0 - C_D^1)$ to R, so as to achieve his highest level of utility.

To consider the simplest case, let the tax system be proportional at rate t. We focus initially on what horizontal equity requires for the recipient, R. To achieve horizontal equity for R, we need to tax him in the same way as any other individual with pretax aggregate consumption (or income) of C_R^1. Therefore, R's post-tax post-transfer consumption should be $C_R^1(1-t)$. For D the situation is complicated by virtue of the fact that he derives satisfaction from R's consumption. Since D is at least as well off at E as he would be if he had been located at M $(C_D^M, 0)$, it is tempting to treat him in the same way as a selfish individual with income, C_D^M—that is, an income equal to the sum of his own and recipient's incomes—and hence to impose on him a negative income effect equal to $t \cdot C_D^M$. This would require that D achieve an equilibrium along the line, $A'N'$. We can perhaps agree that if anything, this will err on the side of treating D too harshly. If we put these two requirements together, complete horizontal equity would be achieved at E' in figure 1.[13]

In light of this, let us consider the outcomes under two alternative tax regimes. The first is the "neutral" regime, in which the tax is calculated on pretransfer magnitudes, where gifts and bequests *as such* are entirely tax free: the tax base is (C_D^0, C_D^0). The second is the Simons regime, under which D is taxed on pretransfer income and R on

113

FIGURE 1
Horizontal Equity Graph

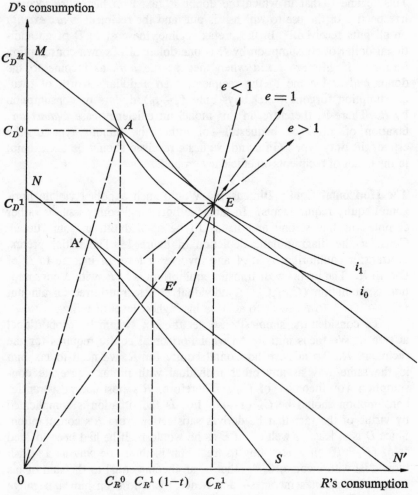

D's consumption

post-transfer income: the tax base is (C_D^0, C_R^1).[14] For each of these tax regimes, we seek to isolate *D*'s post-tax equilibrium and thereby the post-tax income distribution.

To do this, we need to isolate *D*'s choice set, post-tax. This becomes the locus of potential post-tax equilibriums. To begin, for *all* tax regimes, the point A' must lie on *D*'s post-tax consumption possibilities frontier because *D* can always reduce transfers to zero.

Now, under the (C_D^0, C_R^0) tax regime, the relative price to *D* (in terms of own-consumption forgone) of increases in *R*'s consumption

114

remains one dollar, as in the pretax situation. Consequently, D will face a set of potential consumption equilibriums bordered by $A'N'$—precisely what would have been required to achieve horizontal equity with respect to D. The final outcome, however, depends on precisely where D is located on $A'N'$. This in turn depends on D's income elasticity of demand for C_R.[15] In the case where this income elasticity is unity, the post-tax post-transfer equilibrium will be at E': both C_R^1 and C_D^1 will be reduced in the same proportions by the tax. In particular, R's consumption level will be $C_R^1 (1-t)$, precisely as horizontal equity requires. If e exceeds unity, the post-tax post-transfer equilibrium will lie on the line segment $A'E'$ and involve excessively generous treatment of the recipient R.

Let us consider alternatively the (C_D^0, D_R^1) regime recommended by Simons. In this case, the locus of potential post-tax post-transfer equilibriums for D becomes $A'S$, where the slope of $A'S$ is $(1/1-t)$. This is so because the cost to D in own-consumption forgone of a dollar's increase in R's consumption is now $(1/1-t)$ dollars. The actual post-tax post-transfer equilibrium in this case will therefore lie somewhere along $A'S$, and hence will leave D worse off than along $A'N'$. D will be treated excessively harshly. Further, this post-tax post-transfer equilibrium will necessarily involve a lower level of C_R than in the (C_D^0, C_R^0) regime. Unless the donor's income elasticity of demand, e, for recipient's consumption is considerably less than unity, in which case R's post-tax postgift income in the neutral case will be greater than $C_R^1 (1-t)$, this Simons tax arrangement will also tax R too harshly for horizontal equity.

The analysis of relevant cases can be conveniently summarized in table 1. As the table indicates, the policy conclusions are as follows:

• There is no efficiency case for any form of estate/gift taxation whether in the form of separate duties or fully integrated into the income tax in the Simons manner. The neutral arrangement is to leave all gratuitous receipts tax free in the hands of recipients.

• There is no *general horizontal equity* case for any form of estate/gift taxation. A "second-best" argument may be made in the case where the donor's income elasticity of demand for recipient's consumption is less than unity, on the grounds that the income tax on the donor does not "sufficiently" reduce the transfers he makes to the recipient, and hence that the recipient is treated too generously. The horizontal equity advantages in this case are, however, bought at the expense of corresponding horizontal equity disadvantages in terms of excessively harsh tax treatment of donors.

On this basis, we must conclude that the case within the orthodox normative framework for any form of estate and gift duty is extraor-

TABLE 1
HORIZONTAL EQUITY OF ALTERNATIVE GIFT/ESTATE TAX REGIMES

Income Elasticity of Donor Demand	Neutral Regime (C^0_D, C^0_R)		Simons Regime (C^0_D, C^1_R)	
	Donor	Recipient	Donor	Recipient
$e > 1$	Perfectly equitable	Too harsh	Too harsh	Too harsh
$e = 1$	Perfectly equitable	Perfectly equitable	Too harsh	Too harsh
$e < 1$	Perfectly equitable	Too generous	Too harsh	May be equitable

dinarily weak—or at least is so in the absence of definitive empirical evidence indicating that the donor's income elasticity of demand for gifts tends to be low. Casual observation suggests if anything the opposite. (See appendix A.)

Alternative Models of Giving and Their Tax Implications

A natural conclusion of our argument so far is that all estate and gift duties ought to be abolished—and for precisely the reasons of horizontal equity and efficiency that public finance scholars have used in the past to justify such taxes. Estate and gift duties involve a form of double taxation which *violates* horizontal equity and efficiency norms: equity and efficiency considerations require that income be taxed in the hands of donors when received, but *not* taxed again in the hands of recipients if donors choose to pass that income on to others for those others' consumption. The problem with the Simons recommendations is not so much the analytic framework but the analysis itself. Simons and the generations of public finance scholars who have followed him have simply got their logic wrong.

Such a conclusion, though not necessarily unjustified, is a trifle premature. Other models of giving are possible, and these alternative models are not totally implausible. Yet they turn out to have rather different tax implications. Let us examine two other models that seem to merit some consideration and spell out their tax implications.

The (Implicit) Quid Pro Quo Model. One possibility is to deny the existence of genuinely gratuitous receipts. In this event, one argues that everything that passes for a gift in common parlance is merely one side of some (possibly implicit) exchange. A proper modeling of such transfers would include in the utility function of the donor not the well-being of the recipient as such, but the goods or services that the donor receives in exchange for his gift. The Christmas gift that an academic makes to his/her secretary, for example, is to be seen as purchasing loyalty, friendliness, greater conscientiousness, and so on, all with an eye to maximizing the quality of secretarial services received: the gift is, in fact, payment in lieu of wages.[16]

In its most extravagant and imaginative applications this sort of reasoning can be used to explain a very wide variety of apparently altruistic relations. Transfers between spouses are to be viewed as payments for housekeeping, house maintenance, and possibly concubinary services. Transfers from adults to children are to be seen as investments in a contented and secure dotage. And so on.[17]

The difficulty with any such account of giving is that, since the relevant exchange is implicit, one cannot easily tell whether the payment of the gift is in fact contingent on receipt of the relevant goods and services or not. If not, then, of course, the payment is *un*contingent and has to be accounted for in terms other than the exchange model. One cannot, of course, observe that the quid pro quo model applies simply from the fact of *exchange*. The exchange of gifts is entirely consistent with the caring model discussed earlier: it can be explained quite satisfactorily by appeal to the reciprocity of the caring relationship. (I am friendly to those who are friendly to me. One likes to give presents to one's friends. Ergo, one observes the *exchange* of gifts among friends, without either of the parties giving in order that he receives something in return.) The unraveling of all this must await more detailed and extensive empirical work than can be entered into here, even allowing that the matter is one that can be unraveled in principle. Let me simply state my own belief, based on introspection and close observation of a small sample of my own associates, that people *do* give things away without an eye to what they will get in return and that in many cases bequests fit that category.

The Model of the Intrinsic Giver. Even if we allow that giving in a conventional sense does go on, we should note that individuals may give for reasons other than concern for recipients. Consider, for example, the individual who gives as a spiritual discipline, or because it purchases him prestige, or simply because he views himself as the sort of person who gives things away. In such cases, utility accrues primarily from the act of giving in and of itself, and not so much by virtue of concern for any particular recipient. Such an individual would have a utility

117

function of the form: $U_D = f(C_D, T)$, where T is the level of transfers made. This model of giving differs from the caring model examined earlier in that, in this case, the donor derives satisfaction solely from the gifts that he himself makes. An improvement in the lot of the recipient from some *other* source benefits him not at all (whereas, of course, in the caring model the donor rejoices in the good fortune of the recipient—and laments his bad fortune—independently of source).

The absence of any *intrinsic* concern for recipients has important implications for appropriate tax arrangements, specifically:

• In assessing the donor's total consumption possibilities as an input into determining what horizontal equity requires, D's "income" is C_D^0. R's "income" does not effectively increase D's consumption possibilities in the way that it does in the model outlined in figure 1.

• General taxes imposed directly on R do not affect D in any way (again, unlike in the caring model).

On the other hand, taxes imposed on D will affect R to the extent that they reduce D's transfers to R via income effects. The income elasticity of demand for transfers therefore remains a potentially relevant parameter in determining the horizontally equitable tax arrangement[18] (*potentially* relevant, only, for reasons outlined in note 15). Although the analytic differences between this model and the caring model are quite striking, there seems to be considerable difficulty in distinguishing the two cases merely by observation. (The intrinsic giver, for example, might be expected to choose recipients according to their relative worthiness even if such worthiness is very much a marginal consideration in determining how much he gives. In this sense, he may care about the recipients, even though he is an intrinsic giver.) I have nothing in any way decisive to offer in unraveling the prevalence of intrinsic giving as an empirical matter. I do have one conjecture that seems plausible enough, but this I shall save for the next section.

At this point, it may be useful to indicate what orthodox public finance would suggest about tax arrangements in these two alternative models. It seems quite clear that, in the implicit quid pro quo model, all payments that might pass for gifts should be taxed in exactly the same way as labor income—that is after all what they are. In this setting, therefore, the Simons recommendations generate tax treatment that is both neutral and horizontally equitable. Estate and gift duties (integrated on the *acquisitions* side if possible) might well be justified on second-best grounds if the full Simons proposals are administratively unworkable. The Simons scheme, however, remains the conceptual ideal.

In the intrinsic giver model, the conclusions are less direct. The act of transfer is, for the donor, just like any other consumption activity.

The double-taxation feature, that taxes on R are borne by D, characteristic of the caring model, is absent here. Therefore, neutrality seems to require taxation of gifts made in the donor's hands. As in the caring model, this may reduce R's income via income effects on D's transfers to R. Further taxation of gifts in R's hands may therefore not be equitable. In this case, the same conclusions emerge as in the caring model: taxation of gifts and bequests as such is not required.[19]

In the intrinsic giver case, however, there is an interesting wrinkle.[20] Here, neutrality is not necessarily the appropriate efficiency objective. Suppose that the donor's price elasticity of demand for transfers exceeds unity. Then a 10 percent reduction in the price to D of giving will increase gifts to R by more than 10 percent. Therefore, if a subsidy (or tax concession) was applied to gifts made by D, the recipient R could compensate the general taxpayers for the revenue forgone and still be better off. A simple cost-benefit calculation, under equi-revenue assumptions, indicates that both D and R are better off. In this way, one can establish an efficiency case for subsidizing donor giving (and taxing recipients on gifts received, perhaps quite heavily) in the intrinsic giver case.

Estate Duties and Family Status

At this point, we must draw the ends of the analysis together, and focus on the policy issues at stake, as we stated them at the outset. Is there a case for taxing estates and gifts as such *at all*? Is there a case for taxing intrafamily bequests and gifts differently in any way from other forms of giving?

The analytic equipment I have provided to address these issues consists of three possible models of interpersonal giving, all of which might make some claim to empirical relevance and each of which has quite different implications for the proper organization of gifts-and-bequests taxation. How are we to come to a mind on estate/gift duties in the face of this ambiguity?

The first obligation is surely to recognize that ambiguity for what it is. At the very least, the passionate enthusiasm among orthodox public finance scholars for some form of estate taxation receives a severe knock. The Simons recommendations, so resoundingly endorsed by the Carter commission, are revealed to be highly arbitrary and to depend on empirical judgments that tax reform orthodoxy has neither made nor recognized as necessary.

The acknowledgment of ambiguity is not, however, for all its intellectual honesty, very useful in framing policy recommendations. We must finally come to some sort of mind on this matter. We can, I believe, do better, than merely shrug despairingly.

In some ways, Simons's own discussion is instructive here.[21] Simons clearly sensed the ambiguity involved in taxing gratuitous receipts and acknowledged the possibility that his recommendations may "fall well short of fairness as regards donors." (The prospect that recipients may also be excessively taxed seems not to have perturbed him.) Simons was anxious, however, about exempting gratuitous receipts from tax on the grounds that one could thereby open up the prospect of tax avoidance (evasion) on a large scale by inviting taxpayers to disguise ordinary exchanges as gifts. One of his chief objectives was in fact precisely to avoid all those neat problems of motive and mindreading of which earlier writers had made such ado (including Kleinwächter's famous Flugeladjutant's conundrum). He sought "simplicity and elegance" above all (and specifically above matters of finely tuned equity).

Despite his claims to the contrary, however, Simons was more than a little relentless and stubborn on these questions. It seems clear that there are some things one might do to recognize the problems involved here without endangering the entire tax system. It is perfectly obvious, for example, that tips, gratuities, bonuses, and gifts to employees of all types ought to be treated exactly as wages. At the same time, it is surely unpersuasive to argue that relations between husband and wife or between parents and children are essentially identical to those that connect individuals in the marketplace, that purely economic common interest is that which sets the seal on family life. Gifts within the close family seem much more likely to reflect the sort of intrinsic concern for the recipient's well-being that is the central feature outlined in the caring model of giving. If so, gifts, including gifts at death, made within the family *should be entirely exempt from tax*. Equity is achieved by taxing the receipt only once when it is earned as conventional income by the donor. To the extent that one wishes to make some allowance for quid pro quo elements in intrafamily exchanges (and it would be difficult to deny their presence *at all*), then a reasonable compromise might be to have concessional tax treatment of bequests and gifts within the family. My own view is that the logic of the argument here requires such concessions to be extremely generous. On Simons-like grounds of simplicity and elegance, complete exemption has much to recommend it.

Bequests and gifts to charitable institutions represent yet another distinct case, much closer to the intrinsic giver model of transfers. It is certainly difficult to imagine that such gifts represent payments for services rendered by the ultimate recipients as in some normal market exchange. The implicit quid pro quo model seems totally inappropriate here. The possibility that the donor is concerned about the plight of particular recipients seems also, in some cases, fairly remote.[22] There may in such cases be something to be said for concessional treatment of gifts in the hands of donors. Gratuitous *receipts*, however, should be taxed at least as heavily as ordinary income in the hands of *recipients*, perhaps more heavily to offset the cost to revenue of the gift subsidy.

On this basis, the taxation of estates and gifts should ideally be structured as follows:

• Bequests and gifts to charitable institutions, such as independent educational or religious foundations, should earn an income tax concession (or some other subsidy) for donors, but be fully taxed as income to recipients.

• Bequests and gifts (such as those to employees or former employees), where there is some presumption that the gift/bequest is payment in lieu of wages, should be treated Simons-like as income to recipients, with no concession to donors.

• All other bequests and gifts, including specifically those to family members, should be tax exempt to recipients and qualify for no tax on donors apart from income tax payable when the receipts accrue as income (to those donors).

Toward a Theory of the Family Unit

Although this paper could be concluded at this point, I wish to pursue the basic logic a little further, and a little more ambitiously, to spell out some implications for a general theory of the family unit.

As I see it, the central issue in deriving such a theory is the extent to which, if at all, an individual's tax liability ought to be calculated by reference to his/her family status. Let me suggest, on this basis, three reasons why family status might be significant for tax purposes. First, much consumption (housing, transport, entertainment) is undertaken jointly by the family, so that any individual's total consumption depends on the consumption of those joint goods by members of his/her household. This involves a model of the family as a consumption club.

Second, individuals within the family typically receive *transfers* from other members of the family unit—transfers that drive a wedge between the individual's earned "income" and his/her total consumption.

Third, by virtue of the existence of intrafamily transfers, individuals' incentives to take work in the market (and thereby be taxed on income earned *directly*) may be affected. In this case, the main focus of tax policy should be to secure that set of tax rates on market activity which will minimize excess burden (or maximize some explicit social welfare function); this will typically involve for members of single-unit families tax rates different from those for multiple-unit families. It is, as I understand it, this aspect of things on which modern optimal tax theory is

121

focused. This approach tends to be associated with a conception of the family as a firm—a firm that acts so as to maximize the total value of its joint product (including the value of leisure consumed).

These three reasons for the relevance of family status in calculating tax liabilities represent three different possible points of departure for a theory of the family unit. Of these, the first is, I think, entirely misconceived. It is so because forming consumption clubs (or not, as one's tastes for goods versus privacy allow) ought to be irrelevant in determining tax liability. One ignores, and ought to ignore, for tax purposes, whether an individual spends his income on a private swimming pool or joins a swimming club, and whether he owns his own car or uses the local taxi service. Analogously, one ought also ignore whether he enjoys the economics of cohabitation or not. In that sense, all the discussion of equivalence scales in the context of family taxation seems to me to be totally meaningless. The economies of cohabitation are irrelevant for all income redistribution questions.

The third approach is, of course, quite satisfactory as far as it goes. Yet like most of the optimal tax analysis, it seems to ignore much that appears centrally relevant to the more traditional public finance specialist —including the entire horizontal equity thrust which dominates orthodox tax reform advocacy.

As I see it, the second approach is the one that focuses on those centrally relevant matters. The basic question is this: How shall those intrafamily transfers be treated for tax purposes? This is, of course, precisely the issue that has occupied us in this paper. And it is perhaps worth indicating how the various models of giving and their tax implications might translate into a general tax unit policy.

If, for example, one takes the implicit quid pro quo model as the most relevant, then one ought to tax the donor spouse on his/her gross-of-transfer (that is, total earned) income and the recipient spouse on his/her gross-of-transfer income also (that is, total earned income plus transfer). If, for example, consumption of spouses within the family is approximately fifty-fifty, then a couple who earns a total of $30,000 ($20,000 by one spouse and $10,000 by the other) should pay tax as follows: The higher-income spouse pays tax applicable at individual rates on $20,000. The lower-income spouse pays tax applicable at individual rates on $15,000. This arrangement is the only one consistent with the Simons logic, and incidentally with the household-as-firm conception implicit in the optimal tax approach. No tax system in the world, I might add, operates on this basis.

On the other hand, in the conception of the family embodied in the caring model of giving, transfers made within the family are properly tax exempt. They are so for specific analytic reasons, however, and we ought to trace the logic of those reasons properly through a formal treatment of the taxation of the family. We cannot do that here.

We can, however, make an appeal to the analogous caring model, simply by casting D and R as spouses. In doing so, we note that in that model, the reduction in aggregate consumption possibilities associated with taxation for each of D and R is directly related to the *total tax burden which they face between them*. Therefore, how we ought to tax D must take account both of R's income and of the tax imposed on R, and vice versa. The total tax burden that is imposed on D and R together must, of course, take account of the effects on D and R individually. The tax liability that secures horizontally equitable treatment for D will not, in general, secure horizontally equitable treatment for R.

We are therefore faced with a special sort of second-best horizontal equity problem. What the solution to this problem will entail will depend on the desired degree of progressivity in the (individual) tax system, the pretax own-consumption split, and the donor spouse's income elasticity of demand for recipient spouse's consumption. What it does *not* depend on, however, is the particular proportions in which income happens to be *earned*, or on the magnitude of transfers as such—in which sense, it is to be contrasted both with the Simons treatment outlined previously and with any *individual-unit* tax system of the sort currently in use in Australia and Canada (and, one might add, somewhat favored by the avant-garde in public finance circles). Whatever the precise family rate settled on, and however the legal liability to pay that tax is divided between spouses, horizontal equity norms do seem to require *some* form of family unit system. We should also emphasize that the argument here is based on a totally *individualistic* perception of the family and a completely individualistic interpretation of basic horizontal equity norms.

The central conceptual ingredient in generating this theory of family unit taxation is a theory of the appropriate tax treatment of gratuitous transfers. As I see it, this latter theory is the logical starting point for thinking about family unit taxation. This is why what begins in this paper as a discussion of the appropriate tax treatment of bequests properly ends by pointing to the family tax issue more generally—the issue with which this entire conference is to deal.

Appendix A

This appendix deals with the role of income effects in tax analysis, and hence has much broader implications than can be covered here. In the narrower context of the earlier discussion, it should be clear that there is an implicit assumption that the tax/expenditure process leaves the taxpayer worse off ex post. This is in fact a conventional assumption in tax analytics and might be justified in a number of ways:

- Public expenditure may be assumed to be entirely wasteful.
- The tax proceeds might be assumed to be spent on public transfers to third parties in whom D and R have no interest.
- It might be seen as a way of separating out the tax side effects from public spending effects, the latter to be added in at a later step in a *total* analytic procedure.

It must, however, be emphasized that, while this third justification may be acceptable in certain contexts, it is inappropriate here. If public expenditures return to D and R *together* (in almost *any* distribution between them) an amount in public goods benefits equal to the sum of their tax liabilities, then there will be *no* net income effect and the final equilibrium must be at E under the neutral tax regime. The donor, D, will simply adjust his giving to ensure that this is so. If, for example, half the tax revenue goes to each as a demogrant, then R will *not* have a final total income of $C_R^1 (1-t) + \frac{1}{2}t[C_R^0 + C_D^0]$, as the separate analysis would suggest when e is unity. Rather, R's final total income will be C_R^1.

Under the Simons regime, by contrast, there will be a relative price effect due to the double taxation of gifts. The final equilibrium will lie along AE (no net income effects) but above and to the left of E.

In the text, I have made the second assumption, recognizing discreetly in this appendix that it is not necessarily too plausible, and that it *does* make a difference.

Notes

1. Geoffrey Brennan "Second Best Elements of Horizontal Equity Questions," *Public Finance/ Finance Publiques*, vol. 27, no. 3 (1972), pp. 282–91.

2. John Bossons, "The Comprehensive Tax Base as a Goal of Tax Policy," *Journal of Law Economics*, vol. 7 (October 1970), pp. 32–64.

3. Henry Simons, *Personal Income Taxation* (Chicago: University of Chicago Press, 1938), chap. 6. Simons does not rule out the possibility of an additional, though "moderate," estate duty.

4. I defer here to Carl Shoup. See chapter 14 of his *Public Finance* (Chicago: Aldine, 1969), p. 341. The Simons recommendation was of course taken up by the Carter commission (see chapter 14 of volume 3).

5. Shoup, *Public Finance*, p. 342.

6. The main alternative view—that bequests simply represent uncertainty as to the time of death—ignores the obvious point that individuals who wish to maximize lifetime income and leave zero estates can do so by transforming all asset holdings into annuities.

7. This is a very dubious proposition, in my view.

8. See note 6.

9. The discussion here is a rather austere version of an earlier paper on estate duty. Those who desire a more detailed and/or leisurely treatment can consult the earlier version: "Death and Taxes: An Attack on the Orthodoxy," *Public Finance/Finance Publiques*, vol. 33, no. 3 (1978), pp. 201–24.

10. It is for example used extensively in the literature on Pareto desirable redistribution. See, for example, Harold Hochman and James Rodges, "Pareto Optimal Redistribution," *American Economic Review*, vol. 59 (September 1968), pp. 542–54, and George Von Furstenberg and Dennis Mueller, "The Pareto Optimal Approach to Redistribution," *American Economic Review*, vol. 61 (September 1971), pp. 628–34. It is also a model exploited in Gary Becker, "Theory of Social Interactions," *Journal of Political Economy*, vol. 82 (November/December 1974), pp. 1063–95, particularly in section III A.

11. I ignore equi-revenue questions here. There are many taxpayers currently paying income taxes who make no (or negligible) gifts. Hence, we have no requirement that D and R must pay the same aggregate tax between them. If, in toto, the revenue effects of alternative estate tax regimes are negligible (not a bad assumption in fact) then we can ignore the implications for the tax rate of changing the tax regime. We simply consider the tax rate, t, rather than total revenue to be exogenous. The main conclusions are not affected by this assumption.

12. An equivalent effect would be achieved if the donor were exempt from tax on gifts made and the recipient were taxed on gifts received, if the donor's and recipient's tax rates happen to be equal (that is, if taxes are proportional or in the nonproportional case if $C_D = C_R$). In general, this will not be so.

13. Or possibly, if this is viewed as too harsh for D, it would be somewhere along the vertical line above E.

14. An estate/gift tax at rate t gives precisely the same outcome. No distinction between the Simons treatment and the more familiar separate taxation of bequests is necessary here.

15. This income elasticity (e) is defined, as conventionally, by reference to income *effects*. It is thus dependent on changes in C_R^1 which occur in response to changes in what Becker calls "social income," ($C_R + C_D$). That is, $e = [\Delta C_R^1 / C_R^1] \cdot [\Delta (C_R^1 + C_D^1) / (C_R^1 + C_D^1)]$.

16. Under current tax law in most places, such gifts would not attract tax, which may serve to explain why they are so common.

17. See Gary Becker on "The Theory of Marriage: Part II," *Journal of Political Economy*, vol. 82 (March/April 1974), pp. 11–26, and the consequent literature for reasoning along such lines.

18. In this model the income elasticity of demand for transfers (e_T) is measured somewhat more conventionally as: $e_T = (\Delta T/T) \div (\Delta C_D^0/C_D^0)$.

125

19. A somewhat more explicit treatment of this model is contained in "The Incidence of Estate and Gifts Duties: A Theoretical Analysis," in R. Mathews, ed., *State and Local Taxation* (A.N.U. Press, 1977), chap. 3, pp. 39–64.

20. I discuss this wrinkle in more detail in my paper, "Tax Concessions for Charitable Contributions," *Public Finance/Finances Publiques*, vol. 32, no. 3 (1977), pp. 402–11.

21. Simons, *Personal Income Taxation*, chap. 6.

22. A donor who gives to some *philanthropic* enterprise *may* be generally concerned about recipients (for example, the poor, in which case when the poor are made worse off he suffers vicariously). If so, there is some element of pure altruism in his motivations. A donor who gives to an educational foundation, however, presumably would not suffer if the individuals who happened to be the ultimate beneficiaries of his gifts fell on hard times. In many such cases, the donor will not *know* the particular beneficiaries, and will care not at all about them.

Commentary

Richard E. Wagner

Geoffrey Brennan argues primarily that horizontal equity does not support the Haig-Simons proposition that wealth transfers should be treated as income to the donee without an accompanying deduction from the income of the donor. In passing, Brennan also flunks transfer taxation on the basis of efficiency because it distorts the relative price of donor's and donee's consumption.

There are, of course, other efficiency considerations that would also seem to support freedom of gift and bequest. The bias against saving and capital formation in our tax system has been receiving increasing attention. One aspect of this bias is the taxation of wealth transfers, which increases the price to the donor of making such transfers relative to the price of consumption. It is, of course, conceivable that the tax revenues will finance capital accumulation, which means it is conceivable that the global effect of the tax revenues and associated expenditure will be to increase saving and capital formation.

Reality, however, at least as we see it at this time, seems to work in the opposing direction. Hence, the taxation of gifts and bequests will work to increase consumption relative to saving and capital formation. There will, of course, be some rate of tax at which transfers of wealth, though not transfers considered more generally, will disappear entirely. After all, the tax does not erase the bequest motive, but only the constraints within which that motive can operate. To some extent, therefore, other forms of transfer will be substituted for wealth transfers, and with a loss of efficiency ensuing from the substitution of less efficient for more efficient means of transfer, along with the reduction in the capital stock that results from the substitution of donor consumption for wealth transfers.

As for horizontal equity, Brennan argues that application to wealth transfers of the Haig-Simons dictum violates the requirement of equal taxation of equals, at least within the framework of his model. Brennan recognizes that his case is not airtight, for it depends ultimately on the

127

proper model of the donor-donee relation. As his discussion of the quid pro quo and intrinsic giver models shows, it is possible to develop an alternative position, with the quid pro quo model supporting the Haig-Simons position. Brennan argues that his formulation of the donor-donee relation is the more apt one, and I agree with him. Nonetheless, it must be recognized that not all formulations of the donor-donee relation yield his conclusion that the taxation of wealth transfers violates horizontal equity.

There is a sense in which gifts must be viewed as giving utility to the donor, for otherwise they cannot be explained within a utilitarian framework. Within this framework, a donor will apportion his income between transfers and consumption such that the marginal utility per dollar of transfer equals the marginal utility per dollar of consumption. I am troubled, however, by efforts to move from this conceptual point to its implementation in policy, and yet it is this question of implementation that arises when, as in Haig-Simons, it is proposed to treat gifts as income both to the donee and to the donor, and that arises more generally in a variety of questions over the treatment of such nonmarket services as those provided by housewives.

Suppose two people have equal incomes as reflected by the market evaluation of the services they supply, but one of these is philanthropic and the other misanthropic. The philanthropist makes transfers to others and, beyond this, generally receives income of a psychic form from the well-being of others. The misanthropist makes no transfers, and even is worsened by the knowledge of the well-being of others. His psychic income is lowered as the well-being of others increases. If the philanthropist's positive psychic income is said to increase the base for taxation, the misanthropist's negative psychic income must concomitantly be said to decrease it. Haig-Simons includes the former in the tax base, but does not permit an exclusion for the latter. Still, between two people who earn the same income in the market, Haig-Simons would tax the benevolent person more heavily than the malevolent one. Taxes would be piled on a Mother Theresa because of her high psychic income, as compared with a Gary Gilmore.

Although psychic income has use as a conceptual construction, it does not follow that it should be used in matters of tax policy. I would also say the same thing for housewives' services and other kinds of non-market activity. Market relationships are a facet of society, but they do not constitute society. There is more to society than economic relationships. Government too is only a facet of society, and not identical with society. With respect to taxation, government is limited by the extent of market activity. To treat nonmarket activity as if it were market activity, however, is to remove the distinction between economy and

RICHARD E. WAGNER

society by reducing society to economy (or by expanding economy to
society). Simultaneously, since government's tax power is based on
economic activity, government too becomes identical with society, and
with the coming of this identity the idea of a limited government as a
component of society disappears. The state's intrusions would no longer
be limited to the public arena of the marketplace, but could in principle
extend to all aspects of private life. The Haig-Simons proposition,
psychic income, treating activities outside the market as if they were
market activities—all these are contrary to any notion of limited government as an element of a free and well-ordered society.

If there is perhaps any disagreement between Brennan and myself,
it is probably over the importance of concerns of horizontal equity in
transfer taxation. I think most intellectual support for transfer taxation
reflects much more a concern with equalizing starting positions in some
effort to promote equality of opportunity than a concern with horizontal
equity. If life is viewed as a race for riches, transfers of wealth within
the family would seem to give donees from wealthy families a head
start compared with people from other families. The taxation of transfers would in turn seem to be a vehicle for having people start from more
nearly equal starting positions.

On first glance, the argument about equality of opportunity is an
appealing one, but does not seem ultimately to be a very satisfactory
one. When some people are born faster afoot than others, equality of
opportunity is not achieved by having everyone start from the same place,
because the naturally faster ones are advantaged by their genetic endowments. Equality of opportunity requires a system of head starts or
handicaps, such that each person has the same expected time of finish.
In economic life conceived as a race for riches, the taxation of wealth
transfers is a means of reducing the advantages enjoyed by members of
wealthier families. Taxing wealth transfers 100 percent, which is required
by the logic of equality of opportunity, abolishes this source of differential
advantage altogether. The transfer of wealth, however, is only one source
of differential advantage. As suggested earlier, the abolition of wealth
transfers, though inducing some shift from transfers to donor consumption, would also bring about some change in the form of transfers, in
much the same manner that high taxes have induced much economic
activity to be shifted out of the open into the underground economy.
Moreover, genetic endowments, personal values, friends, and numerous
other factors also create differential advantages among people. One
might single out the transfer of wealth for attack because wealth is
relatively visible, but a true concern with equality of opportunity would
also have to look upon these other factors as troublesome, and look for
means to offset them.

129

It is important to understand what ultimately is involved in this common approach to equality of opportunity. For equality of opportunity to be a sensible concern, life must be seen as a race for riches, and once it is, the racing analogy noted previously holds for life as well, and equality of opportunity devolves into equality of outcome, or at least of expected outcome, as I have argued elsewhere.[1] The reason for focusing only on wealth transfers rather than engaging in a complete set of handicaps to equalize expected outcomes is simply the pragmatic one of wealth being more visible and more easily eliminated than the numerous other factors.

I think it is important, though, to understand fully the implications of the inclination to tax wealth transfers as a partial effort to promote equality of opportunity. This can be done most effectively by examining the ideal of equality of opportunity, which in turn must be understood as equality of expected outcome. At base, equality of opportunity is an attack on the family. Parents naturally are partial to their own children, and this partiality will typically find expression in numerous ways, all of which will involve efforts to promote the development and well-being of their children according to the values of the parents. Wealth is only one of many dimensions along which a child's future is influenced by the particular identity of his parents. The more fully equality of opportunity is pursued, the more thoroughly the differentia that results because *particular* children are reared by *particular* parents must be erased. So long as particular children are reared by particular parents, there will be numerous distinctions among children, reflecting the many facets and dimensions of inheritance that the parent-child relationship necessarily involves. Equality of opportunity, then, and the taxation of transfers of wealth within the family as one aspect of an effort to pursue such an objective, represents an attack on the family as the central institution in the process of social reproduction.

There have, of course, been many critics of the family. Plato was one of the earliest and most illustrious. Plato saw the family as competing with the state for people's loyalty. Wishing to see people's loyalties devoted fully to the state, Plato proposed that the family be abolished. Children would be raised communally, so particular parents would not be responsible for and have an interest in the raising of particular children. Without an involvement with and interest in particular children, parents would be equally interested in—that is, indifferent to—all children, as Aristotle subsequently noted. Even though the taxation of wealth transfers would curtail only one aspect of the family relationship, such an effort would gnaw at the importance of the family in society. My suspicion is that an increased taxation of wealth transfers would mostly lead to various other, nontaxed forms of transfer, which would involve relatively more excess burden than weakening of the family. Nonetheless, it seems appropriate to ask wherein lie the benefits of a program that would reduce the ability of parents to express their partiality to their own children. I should think wise policy, which may be simply the absence of any policy, would be that which encouraged the interest of parents in their children, rather than one that weakened it.

In arguing that equality of opportunity reduces to equality of outcome, and that the pursuit of equality of opportunity conflicts with the family as the central unit of society, I would not want to be interpreted as arguing that questions of distributive justice should be dropped from the agenda of public discussion. This is certainly not my position. Indeed, the place of the family in society is a discussable question. An attack on wealth transfers could be limited to the very wealthiest of families. In a free economy I suspect such selective efforts at curtailing wealth transfers would have mainly costs and few, if any, benefits. For one thing, I think there is value to a society from the presence of old wealth. In a free economy the existence of old wealth harms no one, for old wealth can maintain its position only so long as it continues to provide service of value to others in society, for otherwise such wealth will not be replenished.

Of course, ours is not a free economy, though it is probably less unfree than many. In our system of government, legislation is to an important degree sold to the highest bidder, and paid for by taxes extracted from others, as much recent work is beginning to explore. One important feature of such special-interest legislation is its use to forestall competition from newcomers. A substantial component of legislation represents, as it were, the purchase of legislation by established wealth to curtail competition, for the presence of such competition would threaten the positions of some of those already established.

Although we commonly speak of labor and capital as providing the basic dividing line for social conflict, the more appropriate division may well be between established positions that stand to lose by competition and those who would compete with them. Certainly the United Auto Workers union and General Motors, Ford, and Chrysler favor restrictions on foreign imports. Certainly unions and firms in high-cost areas of the nation favor minimum wages to raise the relative cost of production of their competitors in other areas. The list of illustrations could be developed almost interminably. The ultimately correct answer to this use of wealth to secure legislation to maintain sheltered status positions is, I think, to modify existing political institutions in the direction of rewarding more strongly wealth-creating rather than wealth-transferring and wealth-destroying policies.

Alternatively, the selective use of transfer taxation to break down established wealth would reduce the ability of old wealth to maintain its position by purchasing protective legislation. Once the newcomers become successful, however, they will be in a position to purchase protective legislation, and the wealth-eroding facets of contemporary democracy will still be with us. I would rather look to a reform of democratic institutions more in line with the creation of wealth as against its transfer. This becomes especially so once it is recognized that we are simply one nation among many in a generally dangerous world, rather than existing as an isolated state, as most writings on public economics, wealth distribution, and the like presume. That is, policies that promote the creation of wealth would seem more consistent with our survival than policies that promote the erosion of wealth, as wealth transfers do. It is only in the fairy tale world of the isolated state that wealth transfers can be discussed independently of any consideration of survival in the face of rival, predatory nations.

To say this, however, is not to say that questions of distributive justice should be abolished. I think the literature on distributive justice raises vital questions, though I prefer to think of those in positive rather than in normative terms. That is, rather than thinking in terms of a relation between different distributive outcomes or processes and criteria of distributive justice, I prefer to think in terms of a relation between order in society and those outcomes or processes. The literature on distributive justice can be restated as a positive prediction that an orderly, peaceful social existence is inconsistent with certain types of distributive outcomes or processes. Certainly if there are people who might expect to fare as well or better under anarchy than within the existing order, a necessary condition for stability is absent. I might also add that once we think in terms of a network of societies rather than an isolated society, the necessary conditions for order come to include conditions for order among societies as well as within any society. The same questions of wealth creation versus wealth transferral (and wealth destruction) arise, then, in North-South issues, as arise internally.

By now I have come a long way from a consideration of Brennan's paper on transfer taxation. This is perhaps only natural. The taxation of wealth transfers has significance well out of proportion to its importance in our revenue system. Indeed, as a source of revenue, taxes on wealth transfers amount to little more than one percent of all government revenues in the United States. What gives transfer taxation such a disproportionate significance is that it relates directly to the processes by which a society reproduces itself. Brennan's paper is a nice explanation of why a claim of horizontal equity provides at best only weak support for the taxation of wealth transfers. Horizontal equity, however, is only one facet of the general case for taxing wealth transfers. When these other facets are explored, I think they, too, weigh in support of freedom of gift and bequest, thereby reinforcing Brennan's argument.

Exploration of these other facets, however, is a more complex task, which makes firm conclusions more elusive to grasp. Nonetheless, I think it is these other facets that address the most substantial questions surrounding transfer taxation, and at which analysis and discussion in the future can most profitably be directed. Now that Brennan has explained why horizontal equity is a bogus argument for the taxation of wealth transfers, perhaps the attention of scholars will turn more fully to the assessment of the other knottier issues that remain.

Note

1. Richard E. Wagner, "Sense versus Sensibility in the Taxation of Personal Wealth," *Canadian Taxation: A Journal of Tax Policy*, vol. 2 (Spring 1980), pp. 23–30.

Charles Gustafson

Rudy Penner invited me to participate in this seminar on Taxation and the Family. He said that he would like to have the perspective of a lawyer. I was skeptical at first—we in the profession know how we are regarded. Shakespeare said—I think it was in *Midsummer Night's Dream*—that "the lunatic, the lover and the lawyer are, of imagination, quite compact." And, of course, Carl Sandburg asked why the hearse horse snickered when the lawyer's bones went by. So, I was skeptical when Rudy asked. But he did ask, and then mentioned that there would be a free lunch. So I am here to provide a somewhat different perspective—that of the practicing lawyer and counselor.

The lawyer's perspective on estate taxes is marked very symbolically by the extraordinary proliferation of seminars on estate planning. Admittedly, some of these seminars take place in tropical climates in February or on cruise ships in August. It must be conceded that these seminars are often conducted with extraordinary efficiency by those who actually wish to participate. Some lawyers, however, do tend to regard the estate tax as an opportunity. Several years ago, a luncheon speaker at an estate-planning conference asserted that he had compared the number of estates that had come into being during the previous year with the number of people who had attended estate-planning seminars. He concluded from the comparison there were about 0.5 estates that needed to be planned under the then applicable laws for every seminarian who attended an estate-planning seminar.

133

Of course, the beauty of all this from the perspective of my profession is that changes in family status and changes in tax laws mean that there are some estates than can be planned over and over again—all billable at hourly rates—which is one of the reasons why some cynics refer to this last piece of legislation as the "Lawyers and Accountants Economic Recovery Act of 1981."

One perception of mine that differs somewhat from those that have been articulated here is that the estate tax really is born of some very primitive instincts about wealth redistribution. Those of us who are interested in history and anthropology know that in many very basic societies, something like an estate tax was imposed even in situations where no one would have pretended to have created or endeavored to administer something as complex as an income tax. It seemed fair for the society to take a measure of one's wealth at the time of death. Perhaps these instincts are still relevant. It may be that the existence of an estate tax is more important as a political rather than an economic issue.

Let us consider the trend of statutory change regarding estate taxes in the past five years. The Tax Reform Act of 1976 included a number of changes in the estate tax that were at the time regarded as rather radical:

• the integration of the estate tax mechanism and the adoption of the unified credit
• the imposition of a tax on one of the devices that the profession had developed for avoiding what would have appeared to be the full measure of estate tax burdens, as they appeared to exist in the statute—that is, the tax on generation-skipping transfers
• the automatic inclusion of gifts that had been made during the three years before death without resort to any particular evidentiary concerns

Of course, there were some benefits from the point of view of the taxpayer. The effective rates of tax were reduced. The marital deduction was liberalized. There were certain valuation benefits created for small businesses.

There were some technical changes in 1978 that were important to those in the category of taxpayers affected. The summer of 1981, however, brought another round of radical changes in the estate tax which seem to indicate a very strong trend in support of the proposition that the estate tax as a political device is at least of diminishing importance.

I am sure that you have examined at least the outlines of that act. No publication appears today without a story about it. After a six- or seven-year transition period, the taxable estate is not going to be one that is worth $175,000, but rather one that is worth $600,000. The maximum rate of tax is eventually going to be reduced from 70 percent to 50 percent. Limits on the amount of the marital deduction will be eliminated, an action that gives rise to many inferences about the relationships that we have been discussing today. There are new rules about jointly held property. The annual gift exclusion is going to provide an opportunity for married couples to give $20,000 a year to each of their children.

So, it seems to me from a practical point of view that the trend is relatively clear. This trend may well mean that the principal relevance of estate taxes for this society will be a profession continually devoted to the creation of opportunities for avoiding the tax, but only for still wealthier families, along with the continued development of complex devices and arrangements to avoid the imposition of tax for those families.

Most important, from a political and economic point of view, there is an income tax issue that has been inextricably interwoven with the congressional treatment of estate taxes. The issue was squarely addressed in 1976 as part of the Tax Reform Act. The estate tax reductions were accompanied by a provision for carry-over of basis for assets transferred at death. That is to say, the cost of assets to the decedent would be used by the heirs for calculating future capital gains taxes instead of the value at death as in current law. The effective date of that major change was deferred to 1978, and then postponed again. President Carter—having made the observation while campaigning that the income tax system was an embarrassment to civilized man—indicated that he would veto any attempt to eliminate the carry-over basis provisions. When repeal of carry-over basis appeared as an integral part of the windfall profits tax legislation in 1980, however, it was quickly recognized (as I understood it) as an essential aspect of the energy program, and therefore had to be accepted.

We will recall as well that by 1980 the bar, the accounting profession, and the bankers had convinced everyone who mattered that it would be quite impossible for taxpayers to do anything as complex as finding out what the cost of an asset might have been. If we are to examine fully the conceptual premises of the taxation of property transfers at death, it seems to me inescapable that we must consider as well this peculiar opportunity (created by the step-up in basis) for the avoidance of any tax on certain kinds of income.

Although it has not been asserted here, a strong case can be made that the estate tax is no longer justifiable on any economic grounds. In practice it does not serve importantly to redistribute wealth. Its revenue impact is marginal. Perhaps the psychological and political considerations are sufficient to justify a continuation. The practical im-

135

pact of estate tax, however, may well be to foster convoluted financial arrangements. That is not all bad news. There will be more seminars for estate planners. There may be more fodder for fiction by folks like Louis Auchincloss and John O'Hara, who occasionally write about tangles in wealthy families' estate planning. And—in my experience—it will probably continue to create occasional embarrassment and some frustration on the part of younger clan members who would like to inquire as to estate tax avoidance plans on the part of elder clan members without appearing to display an unseemly form of death wish.

Finally, there seems to be at least one lesson clearly taught by the recent reduction in estate taxes. There is an exception to supply-side economic theory. As far as one can determine presently, the reduced estate tax burden will not serve as an incentive to increase the number of deaths per capita in the society—despite the extraordinary possibilities that are created by the apparently growing horde of born-again taxpayers.

Discussion Summary

Carl Shoup suggested that Simons did not fully distinguish between two concepts of income. On the one hand, income could be considered to be anything that increases well-being. No economic activity need be involved. On the other hand, the concept could be narrowed to refer only to well-being associated with economic activity—that is, the use of factors of production. Simons seemed to be using the first concept in discussing the taxation of gifts, but he did not follow through with the logical implications of this approach. If he had, he would have advocated the taxation of leisure.

Geoffrey Brennan responded that his own view was consistent with Shoup's second-income concept that relates income to factor activity, but that he did not believe that Simons accepted such a narrow concept.

Joseph Pechman asked Brennan to respond to Richard Wagner's point that there was a political desire to redistribute wealth and that a failure to recognize this represented a glaring omission from Brennan's paper. Brennan responded that he did not believe that society considered it to be inequitable to fail to tax estates. He noted that estate taxes were disappearing around the world. Although there was some appeal to the notion that it was inequitable for individuals to inherit large amounts of wealth, Brennan felt that the logical implication of that notion is unsettling. It would seem to imply, he said, that it was preferable for wealthy individuals to consume their wealth before death so that nothing would be bequeathed to succeeding generations.

It was suggested that there might be an efficiency argument for estate taxation. It is difficult for society to redistribute income without creating work and saving disincentives, and taxing wealth transfers at death might be a more efficient means of raising revenue while attaining some measure of equality. Brennan replied that it may be more efficient to tax away all wealth, just as lump-sum taxes may be efficient, but such approaches are not popular, because it is necessary to place more weight on equity and fairness.

Some members of the audience believed that transfers of wealth created a negative externality in the sense that it made it more difficult

137

to run a "just" society. The point was made several ways. It was argued that there was no reason not to tax someone who acquired wealth with no expenditure of effort. Brennan replied that this was a question of property rights. He saw no reason to believe that society at large has a claim on assets that a person wishes to transfer to someone else.

Social Security and the Family

Virginia P. Reno and Melinda M. Upp

This conference focuses on horizontal-equity questions involving the treatment of individuals and families in the tax structure. Similar types of questions are raised about the social security benefit structure. Which units should be treated alike? Is the appropriate unit of comparison the individual worker or the worker and his or her family? Married couples in which both the husband and the wife work have expressed dissatisfaction with the personal income tax because they pay more than if they were unmarried. The comparison that here gives rise to the so-called marriage penalty issue is between married and unmarried workers. Under social security, married couples in which both husband and wife have worked sometimes express dissatisfaction because their combined benefits can be less than those paid to a one-earner couple with the same combined earnings. The comparison that creates the issue here is between one- and two-earner couples.

With both social security and the personal income tax, questions about who should be treated alike become an issue because some group is dissatisfied with the treatment it receives. Income tax issues arise when one group feels its taxes are too high relative to another's. Social security issues arise when one group feels its benefits are too low relative to another's. Ways to address such issues can take either of two forms:

- incremental change—that is, approaches that alter one or two features of a system to mitigate the dissatisfaction
- comprehensive approaches—that is, fundamental restructuring of the system to incorporate new principles about who gets treated alike

Virginia P. Reno is acting director of the Program Analysis Staff in the Social Security Administration's Office of Policy. Melinda M. Upp is an analyst on the staff, The authors wish to thank Jane Ross, Mary Ross, and Lawrence H. Thompson for their comments on an earlier version of this paper, but note that the views expressed here are strictly their own and do not necessarily represent those of the commentators or of the Social Security Administration.

The comprehensive approach often has more theoretical appeal. Incremental change, however, allows a smoother transition, minimizes unintended side effects, and retains accepted features of the existing system.

The provisions of the Economic Recovery Tax Act of 1981 on the income tax treatment of families are an example of the incremental approach for mitigating the so-called marriage penalty of concern to two-earner couples. The working-spouse deduction and the increased child care credits were enacted to provide relief to two-earner couples without changing the basic framework of the tax system. A comprehensive approach could have totally eliminated the marriage penalty by shifting from the family to the individual as the unit for taxation and then ignoring marital status or spouse's income in taxing each individual. To ignore marital status, however, is also to ignore the economic well-being that dual-earner couples derive from their combined income. A comprehensive approach that ignored family income could have generated new issues of fairness between singles and two-earner couples. The incremental approach, in contrast, reduced the marriage penalty while retaining family income as the tax base and minimizing the creation of new issues of fairness.

In the 1970s comprehensive proposals were made to restructure family benefits in the social security system. The two most widely discussed options were earnings sharing and a double-decker plan. These proposals incorporated new principles about who should be treated alike. They also appealed to those who thought benefits for divorced women, widows, homemakers, or working wives should be made more adequate. This paper finds that earnings sharing, the comprehensive approach that achieved the most popularity, may not be as successful as some of its supporters hoped in raising the level of benefits paid to various groups of women. In addition, it could create new equity dilemmas and would sacrifice aspects of the current system that many find appealing.

The first section of this paper describes the basic features of the current system, including earnings replacement, protection offered to spouses and survivors of workers, and treatment of divorced spouses. The second section traces the evolution of issues about present family benefits. It shows how issues that began with concern about the level of benefits for various groups of women evolved into new principles about who should be treated alike with regard to: one- and two-earner couples, survivors of such couples, homemakers and paid workers, and divorced persons. The principles that emerged seemed to argue for a comprehensive change such as earnings sharing.

Another section describes a report, *Social Security and the Changing Roles of Men and Women*, issued by the Department of Health, Education, and Welfare in 1979, and presents the report's analysis of the earnings-sharing and double-decker plans. The discussion notes that the double-decker plan failed to attract a constituency and then describes the early attraction and subsequent disenchantment of the 1979 Advisory Council on Social Security with the earnings-sharing concept as council members realized the magnitude of the plan's effects both on one-earner couples and on popular aspects of the social security system. It presents the council's two-part recommendation for limited earnings sharing that was intended to raise benefits for divorced women and widows, and it reports on subsequent staff analysis indicating that the proposals would not help those groups as much as the council had hoped and would, in turn, create new equity dilemmas.

A final section describes various incremental changes that, unlike comprehensive reforms, could address specific types of dissatisfaction with benefit levels and could be scaled to reflect the availability of program resources. It describes the recommendation of the National Commission on Social Security to mitigate concern about low benefits for working women by allowing child care credits toward the special minimum benefit, and it notes other relatively modest changes in spouse benefits or survivor benefits to mitigate dissatisfaction with benefits for two-earner couples relative to one-earner couples.

The Present System

Social Security is usually described as a system for partially replacing earnings lost when a worker becomes disabled, retires, or dies. Several critical aspects of the system are implicit in this statement.

Benefits for Workers. Most fundamentally, the system is based on individual workers. Taxes from workers' earnings are matched by their employers and used to finance benefits. In 1981, the payroll tax rate for cash benefits was 5.35 percent of earnings, up to $29,700 for employees and employers each.[1]

The insured risks for which workers' benefits are paid are loss of earnings due to retirement or disability. In the original Social Security Act, no retirement benefits were paid to the worker who had any earnings from regular covered employment. A less stringent test of retirement, or earnings test, remains in the law today.[2]

Eligibility for disability benefits, which were added in 1956, is also defined in terms of inability to earn. A worker is found disabled only if he or she has a severe medical impairment and, because of that impairment, is unable to engage in substantial gainful work.

141

TABLE 1

EFFECTS OF BENEFIT FORMULA FOR WORKERS REACHING AGE SIXTY-TWO IN 1981

Average Indexed Monthly Earnings (AIME) ($)	Primary Insurance Amount (PIA) ($)	PIA/AIME Ratio (%)
300	218	72.8
400	250	62.5
500	282	56.5
600	314	52.4
700	346	49.5
800	378	47.3
900	410	45.6
1,000	442	44.3
1,100	474	43.2
1,200	506	42.2
1,300	534	41.1
1,340	540	40.3

NOTE: Benefits are reduced by 20 percent if claimed at age sixty-two. Benefits are increased by the cost of living at and after age sixty-two. These adjustments (including that for June 1981) are not reflected in the table. The maximum AIME for a worker age sixty-two in 1981 was $1,340.

SOURCE: Authors' calculations.

The earnings replacement principle of the present system is also evident in the benefit computation. The size of a worker's basic benefit is determined by his or her average past earnings. Earnings are averaged over a long and increasing period since 1950. For those reaching age sixty-five in 1981, earnings were averaged over the highest twenty-two years. For those now under age fifty-three, retirement benefits are scheduled to be based on earnings averaged over their highest thirty-five years. A worker's past earnings are indexed to reflect prevailing economy-wide wage rates near age sixty-two or the onset of disability, if earlier. The worker's average indexed monthly earnings (AIME) are then used to compute the basic benefit.

The benefit formula applied to a worker's AIME is weighted to replace relatively more of past earnings for low earners than for high earners.[3] The results of the formula for workers reaching age sixty-two in 1981 are shown in table 1.[4] At present, a sixty-two-year-old who had always earned about the average economy-wide wage would have average indexed monthly earnings of about $960. The benefit, before any

TABLE 2
REPLACEMENT RATES UNDER THE 1935 AND 1939 ACTS AND
UNDER PRESENT LAW
(percent)

Level of Wage Earned	1935 Act		1939 Act		Present Law
	First year	Long term	First year	Long term	Long term 1990
Average	20	58	29	40	41
Minimum	30	73	41	57	52
Maximum	10	34	17	23	27

NOTE: Benefits are given as a percentage of final earnings.
SOURCE: Robert J. Myers, *Social Security,* 2nd ed. (Homewood, Ill.: Richard D. Irwin, 1981), p. 262.

reduction for early retirement or adjustment of cost-of-living increases after age sixty-two, would replace about 45 percent of those average earnings.

A special minimum benefit for workers is based on their number of years of coverage, rather than their average indexed earnings. The benefit is intended for long-service, low-paid workers and is paid only if it is greater than the benefit under the regular formula. Only about 1 percent of retired workers now receive the special minimum.[5]

Introduction of Family Benefits. The original Social Security Act provided monthly benefits only to retired workers and lump sum payments to survivors under certain circumstances. In 1939, before any monthly benefits were actually paid, the act was amended to provide monthly survivor benefits to widows and children and supplemental benefits to wives and children of retired workers. The 1939 amendments also moved up the first payment date for benefits from January 1942 to January 1940 and changed the basic benefit computation for retired workers to increase benefits in the early years of the program and to reduce benefits for long service.[6]

The 1939 changes in the benefit formula for workers are illustrated in table 2, showing replacement rates (benefits as a percentage of final earnings) in the first year and over the long term for low-, average-, and high-earning workers. Both the 1935 and the 1939 acts reflect the earnings replacement principle and the weighted formula for low-paid workers. Under the 1935 formula, replacement rates would have been very low in the early years of the program, but would have risen substantially over the long term for workers who spent a full work life under the system. The 1939 amendments lowered these long-term replacement rates to levels that are not very different from those today. Replacement rates in the early years remained well below these levels, but were higher than those provided in the 1935 act.

Benefits for wives. The wife's benefit—equal to 50 percent of the worker's primary benefit—was added in 1939 to provide additional benefits in the early years where the need was thought to be greatest— that is, for workers whose wives did not receive retired worker benefits. Those workers were assumed to have a greater need than single workers with the same average earnings. According to the 1938 Advisory Council, whose recommendations provided the blueprint for the 1939 amendments: "Payment of supplementary allowances to annuitants who have wives over 65 will increase the average benefit in such a manner as to meet the greatest social need with the minimum increase in cost."[7]

Under the 1939 act, as under present law, a wife's benefit was paid only to the extent that it exceeded her own benefit as a worker. Congress recognized that many wives would earn retired worker benefits in their own right and therefore believed that the ultimate cost of the wife's benefit would be small:

> Because most wives, in the long run, will build up wage credits on their own account, as a result of their own employment, these supplementary allowances will add but little to the ultimate cost of the system. They will, on the other hand, greatly increase the adequacy and equity of the system by recognizing that the probable need of a married couple is greater than that of a single individual.[8]

This projection is borne out by current long-range cost estimates. Based on the assumptions in the 1981 report of the board of trustees of the Old-Age, Survivors and Disability (OASDI) Trust Funds, the long-range average cost of retired-worker benefits is estimated to be about 9.9 percent of taxable payroll, of which 4.33 is for retired women and 5.57 percent for retired men. The cost of benefits for spouses of retired workers is 0.53 percent of payroll.[9]

There have been relatively few changes in the wife's benefit since it was first enacted in 1939. Reduced benefits, equal to 37.5 percent of the worker's Primary Insurance Amount (PIA), are now available to wives at age sixty-two. Spouse's benefits are now also available to husbands of retired women, though few men receive them because their own benefits are almost always higher.

Benefits for aged widows. Some form of protection for survivors has always been a part of the social security system. The 1935 act provided only lump sum payments. The 1939 act provided monthly benefits to children and their widowed mothers and to aged widows. The widow's benefit then payable at age sixty-five was 75 percent of the worker's basic benefit. Various advisory groups over the years expressed concern about the low incomes of aged widows and recommended increases in their social security benefits. In 1961 Congress raised the aged widow's benefit payable at age sixty-two to 82.5 percent of the worker's benefit. The 1963 President's Commission on the Status of Women, the 1968 Advisory Council on the Status of Women, and the 1965 and 1971 advisory councils on social security all recommended that the widow's benefit be raised to 100 percent of the worker's age-sixty-five benefit. It was argued that the widow's needs were no less than the worker's should he have outlived his wife. This change was made in 1972. The widowed spouse benefit is now 100 percent of the worker's benefit if claimed at age sixty-five or later. It is reduced to 82.9 percent if claimed at age sixty-two, and to 71.5 percent if claimed at age sixty (and graduated amounts at other ages between sixty and sixty-five). Similar benefits are now payable to aged widowers. As with the spouse's benefit, the widow(er)'s benefit is paid only to the extent it exceeds the survivor's own benefit as a worker.

Benefits for divorced women. The 1939 amendments made no special benefit provision for divorced women. Divorced women, like all other women and men, would be eligible for benefits based on their own earnings, but they were not eligible for spouse's or survivor's benefits. Subsequent amendments extended to many divorced women the types of benefits payable to wives and widows.

The first provision for divorced women was enacted in 1950 when widowed mother's benefits were extended to divorced women who had in their care entitled children of the deceased former husband. There was no special duration-of-marriage requirement for a young divorced mother, but there was a special proof-of-dependency requirement. She had to show that she was receiving one-half of her support from the former husband before he died.

Concerns about gaps in protection for aged divorced women were raised in the 1960s. The 1963 President's Commission recommended that wives' and widows' benefits be extended to divorced women who had had long marriages. This was done in 1965, subject to a twenty-year duration-of-marriage requirement and a dependency test. In 1972 the dependency requirement was eliminated, and in 1977 the duration requirement was shortened to ten years.

In summary, the system now provides the following benefits in old age:

145

- primary benefits for retired workers based on their lifetime earnings from which social security taxes were paid
- supplemental benefits to spouses of retired workers if the spouse's benefit exceeds the spouse's own retired-worker benefit
- survivor's benefits to aged widows and widowers, if the survivor's benefit—of up to 100 percent of the deceased worker's benefit—exceeds the widow(er)'s own retired-worker benefit
- for divorced persons whose marriages lasted ten years, benefits like those that would be paid had the divorce not taken place

These features are integral to the present social security system and to a large extent account for its popularity among broad segments of American society. Yet within these features lie also the seeds of the dissension that was to arise in the 1970s as various groups, concerned about relative benefit levels, added their voices to those who sought higher absolute levels of benefits for certain groups.

Evolution of Issues

As is evident in the foregoing discussion, past changes in social security family benefits were intended to address concerns about absolute adequacy. This type of concern continued to be raised in the 1960s and 1970s. Two new elements were introduced into the debate during this period, however: concern about the level of benefits paid to some, relative to the level of benefits paid to others, and concern about the notion of dependency perceived to be implicit in the way protection is provided for homemakers.[10]

This section will trace the evolution of these concerns about the absolute and relative levels of benefits as they pertain to four groups of women—working wives, widows, homemakers, and divorced spouses—and the way in which discussion of new philosophical issues about who should be treated alike came to dominate the debate.

Working Wives. Concerns about working wives were raised in the early 1960s, as women who had worked during World War II began to retire, and as the mothers of the baby boom entered the work force in increasing numbers. The Committee on Social Insurance and Taxes of the 1963 President's Commission on the Status of Women was one of the first public panels to look at the treatment of the working wife not only in absolute terms but also relative to noninsured wives and to other workers. The committee concluded, as others had done before and would do later, that in many ways working wives are treated fairly. The committee's report noted that working wives:

• like other workers, receive benefits on their own earnings that represent more than the actuarial equivalent of their own contributions
• often do receive higher benefits on their own earnings than as wives
• are protected from the full effect of having gaps in their own earnings because the benefit formula is weighted
• have some protections not available to noninsured wives, such as disability protection, survivor's protection for their children, and retirement benefits that are independent of the husband's work status[11]

The committee concluded, however, that the feelings of injustice had to be acknowledged and that some increase in benefits for working wives could be justified:

> Nevertheless, the feeling of the working wife that she should receive more in benefits than the nonworking wife has some merit. Not only have both she and her husband contributed to the program, but the fact that she has had earnings also means that the family unit suffers a greater loss in income on retirement than if only the husband had worked.[12]

The committee recommended that the working wife's spouse's benefit be offset against her benefit based on her own work record by $1 for $2 instead of $1 for $1. The wife's benefit, then, would be reduced to zero only when her own benefit equaled or exceeded her husband's. (Now the wife's benefit is reduced to zero when her worker's benefit equals half the husband's PIA.)

The committee's plan at that time would have cost 0.15 percent of taxable payroll if, as the committee recommended, it applied only to wives, not to widows. The full Commission on the Status of Women did not endorse the proposal. In the late 1960s, a new dimension was added when the issue was cast not only in terms of working versus nonworking wives but also in terms of one-earner couples versus two-earner couples with the same combined earnings.

Like the 1963 committee, the 1968 Task Force on Social Insurance and Taxes of the Citizens' Advisory Council on the Status of Women cited concern about the need for working wives to receive more, based on their own social security earnings, relative to nonworking wives. The task force went further, however, in charging that an inequity existed between couples: "[A]n anomalous situation is created whereby an aged couple may get less in total monthly benefits if both the man and wife worked than a couple getting benefits based on the same total earnings where only the husband worked."[13] The present system does not pay equal benefits to couples with the same combined earnings. Table 3 shows benefits under present law for different levels of combined earnings. The 1968 task force thus recommended a proposal to equalize benefits

147

TABLE 3
BENEFITS FOR A ONE-EARNER COUPLE AND A TWO-EARNER COUPLE
UNDER PRESENT LAW, 1981

| | Couple's Combined Full Monthly Benefits ($) | |
Couple's Combined Average Indexed Monthly Earnings ($)	One-earner couple (150% PIA)	Two-earner couple (each spouse earned half of combined AIME)
400	376	360
600	472	437
800	568	501
1,000	664	565
1,200	760	629
1,340	810	673

NOTE: The table gives full benefit amounts if both husband and wife claimed benefits at age sixty-five. The cost-of-living adjustment of June 1981 is not reflected in these figures.
SOURCE: Authors' calculations.

paid to one- and two-earner couples by "leveling up"—that is, by raising the level of benefits paid to two-earner couples. The specific concept endorsed by the task force was the use of couples' earnings as a base for computing couples' benefits, a concept incorporated into a bill introduced in Congress in 1967 by Representative Martha Griffiths. The Griffiths bill in 1968 was estimated to cost 0.52 percent of taxable payroll.[14]

The task force noted, however, that "the long-run solution may take a different approach" and recommended consideration of a double-decker approach:

Realizing the "social" aspects of the system with respect to lower paid workers and workers with dependents, we recommend for the consideration of the next Advisory Council on Social Security a system that would (1) provide for meeting their social needs through a socially adequate benefit financed out of general revenues and (2) provide for supplementation of this basic benefit by contributory wage-related benefits for those who worked in covered employment.[15]

The labor member of the task force objected to the double-decker approach, arguing that a benefit financed from general revenues could become subject to a means test. The labor representative also objected

148

to the combined-earnings plan because raising benefits for workers who are married to each other could generate new issues of fairness with regard to single workers. The "marriage bonus" for workers who are married might also be viewed as a "singles' penalty" for those who are not married.

Throughout the 1970s, various groups continued to advocate raising benefits for working wives and/or equalizing benefits between one- and two-earner couples with the same combined earnings. New voices also joined the debate, however, casting these issues in slightly different ways. Sometimes they espoused similar-sounding principles to promote quite different results:

• Some, as will be noted later, wanted to eliminate the notion of the "dependency" of wives. They wanted to recognize a homemaker's economic contribution to the marriage by equalizing benefits between spouses in a marriage. Some of the early proponents of this view were more concerned with equalizing benefits within the couple, rather than between one- and two-earner couples.

• Others also wanted to eliminate "dependency," but favored achieving it by phasing out spouse's benefits. Early proponents of this view were more concerned with improving the treatment of working wives relative to nonworking wives than with equalizing benefits between one- and two-earner couples.

• Some favored equalizing benefits between one- and two-earner couples and were willing to accept a relatively high cost to achieve that end. They argued for approaches that leveled up by raising benefits for two-earner couples. Some such plans included raising benefits for single workers, so as to avoid creating a "singles" issue.

• Others also favored equalizing benefits between one- and two-earner couples, but advocated leveling down benefits for one-earner couples as a way to achieve that end without increasing costs or generating new issues of fairness between couples and single workers.

Many of these disparate viewpoints ultimately found an element of agreement in the statement that *couples with the same combined past earnings should have the same combined retirement benefits.* This principle was not reflected in the existing social security system.

Widows. Groups expressing concern about survivors' benefits were not as disparate as those advocating improved benefits for working wives, but they did represent two distinct views: those who wanted to raise the absolute level of widow's benefits and those who wanted to equalize the level of benefits paid to survivors of one-earner couples and two-earner couples.

149

TABLE 4

BENEFITS FOR SURVIVORS OF ONE-EARNER COUPLES AND
TWO-EARNER COUPLES, 1981

Couple's Combined Average Indexed Monthly Earnings ($)	Survivor's Full Monthly Benefit ($)	
	One-earner couple	Two-earner couple (each spouse earned half of combined AIME)
400	251	180
600	314	218
800	378	251
1,000	442	282
1,200	506	314
1,340	540	337

NOTE: The table shows the full benefit at age sixty-five if neither the survivor nor the deceased spouse claimed early retirement benefits. The cost-of-living adjustment of June 1981 is not reflected in these figures.
SOURCE: Authors' calculations.

The first group supported increases in survivors' benefits that were enacted in the 1960s and 1970s. Those amendments, however, did not address the fact that for a given level of combined earnings, survivors of one-earner couples receive more than survivors of two-earner couples, as shown in table 4. Thus, those who argued that couples with like earnings should be treated alike also argued that *survivors of couples with the same combined earnings should be treated alike.*

Because of relatively high poverty rates among aged widows, there was little sustained interest in applying this principle by lowering widow's benefits. If the equalization principle was to be met, then, benefits for survivors of two-earner couples would have to be increased. The most commonly proposed method of achieving this goal was to permit widows and widowers to receive benefits based in some way on the couple's combined earnings.

Homemakers. In the 1970s, various advisory groups and women's organizations advocated that social security explicitly recognize the value of work performed by homemakers. It was argued that so-called dependents' benefits were demeaning and should be replaced with independent credits for homemakers.

In 1976, the National Commission on the Observance of International Women's Year recommended that "the homemaker be covered in her own right under Social Security to provide income security to the risk of old-age, disability and death." The commission further recommended "that the Secretary of HEW be directed to give high priority to developing an Administration proposal achieving this purpose."[16]

The commission reported that its recommendation would enhance the status of homemakers and avoid the notion of dependency. It favored homemaker credits that would provide (1) disability protection for homemakers, (2) higher benefits for women with careers divided between child care and paid work, and (3) higher benefits for divorced women that are independent of the former husband's status. The issue, however, was cast in terms of the guiding principle of independent recognition of homemakers' work, rather than the particular results. It was implied that homemakers should receive at least the level of benefits that the present system provides. It was thought, however, that those benefits should stem from independent credits. The new principle seemed to be to *treat homemakers like paid workers and eliminate "dependents'" benefits.*

Divorced Persons. The rising divorce rate since the mid-1960s focused attention on the problems of divorced women, not only with regard to social security but also with respect to other federal programs and state laws regarding property rights. Women divorced in mid-life or in old age often had low incomes and few opportunities for improving their status. Divorced women expressed concern over their low benefits under social security and over the fact that a spouse's benefit is not paid until the worker retires.

The treatment of divorce per se posed a dilemma. In the current system, divorced spouses are treated as if they were still married, provided they meet the duration-of-marriage requirement. This approach was criticized, however, because divorced women's situations are different from those of wives. For divorced nonworking retired women, the spouse's benefit was not a supplement to a partner's benefit. It was the only benefit. Although it seemed reasonable to link payment of the wife's benefit to the worker's retirement, this was a problem for those older divorced women whose former husbands did not retire and did not support them. Yet to pay higher benefits to divorced women than to wives would have created a so-called divorce bonus or marriage penalty because divorced women would be treated more favorably than those who remained married.

One solution was to regard marriage as a partnership of equals. The National Women's Conference, held in Houston, Texas, in November 1977 adopted the following resolution: "The Federal Government and State legislatures should base their law relating to marital and property,

151

inheritance and domestic relations on the principle that marriage is a partnership in which the contribution of each spouse is of equal importance and value." [17]

The partnership principle thus provided a new principle for social security reform proposals: *at divorce, treat both parties alike.* Again, support for the principle was gained from both those who were concerned about the relative level of benefits available to divorced workers and their ex-spouses and those who wanted to raise the absolute level of benefits available to divorced women.

Although few married women were objecting to the fact that their own benefits were less than their husband's or that the wife's benefit could not be received until the husband retired, it became clear that to offer benefits to divorced women that were not available to wives could be perceived as a divorce bonus. Thus, it was necessary to apply the partnership principle to married persons in order to *treat married and divorced persons alike and thereby remain neutral with regard to divorce.* This had the coincident effect of ensuring that partners in intact marriages would be treated alike.

In sum, then, a new set of principles was embraced, both by those who wanted to improve the absolute level of benefits for many individual women, as well as by those who believed that the social security system should reflect new principles about who should be treated alike between one- and two-earner couples and between their survivors, between husbands and wives, between homemakers and workers, between divorced spouses, and between married and divorced persons. It was hoped that the adequacy concerns could be achieved in the course of implementing the new principles and that the new principles could coexist with existing aspects of the social security system for which there was, and continues to be, broad-based support.

Comprehensive Change

As was described previously, a disparate set of concerns about the social security system found their expression in a new set of principles about who should be treated alike—specifically, that:

- Couples with the same combined earnings should be treated alike.
- Survivors of couples with the same combined earnings should be treated alike.
- Homemakers should be treated like paid workers, and "dependents' " benefits should be eliminated.
- At divorce, both parties should be treated alike in order to reflect the principle of marriage as a partnership of equals.

152

- Married people should be treated like divorced people in order to remain neutral with regard to divorce.

Among those supporting these new principles were those who hoped that benefits could be increased, in absolute terms, for widows, divorced women, working wives, and homemakers.

These principles underlay the development and analysis of the comprehensive options—an earnings sharing plan and a double-decker plan that incorporates certain earnings sharing features—presented in the 1979 Department of Health, Education, and Welfare (HEW) report, *Social Security and the Changing Roles of Men and Women*.[18] The report also discussed more limited options. The principles were taken as a given; the analytic exercise was to see how they could be achieved.

Double-Decker Approach. The double-decker system is used in several foreign countries, including Canada, New Zealand, and Sweden, where social security first took the form of a flat, universal pension paid to all upon the attainment of a certain age without regard to past contributions, earnings, or tests of means. These countries, while retaining the universal first deck, have since added a second deck of benefits that are paid on the basis of prior earnings and contributions. Under the system most commonly discussed in the United States, the second deck would be some flat proportion of AIME, say, 30 percent. The universal flat amount would be financed from general revenues.

The double-decker approach was considered in detail by the 1979 Advisory Council on Social Security. It was favored by four council members who believed that it would clarify the structure of the social security system and the extent to which benefits are weighted for lower earnings and for family size and that it would facilitate public debate over the system's most appropriate emphases.

The double-decker approach was not designed to address concerns relating to women's benefits. Its proponents, however, argued that it could easily be modified by earnings sharing at divorce and provisions for survivors' benefits based on couples' combined earnings. The approach would

- treat alike couples with the same combined earnings
- treat alike survivors of couples with the same combined earnings
- through its first deck, provide all persons, including homemakers, with independent protection and thereby eliminate "dependents' " benefits for spouses
- through earnings sharing at divorce, treat both parties alike

Opposition to the double-decker concept came primarily from two groups. Some feared that the first deck would be means-tested and

153

therefore provide an inadequate alternative to present-law spouse's benefits and weighted benefits for workers. Others feared that the first deck would not be means-tested, but rather that Congress would succumb to pressure to increase it, and that the first deck therefore would become a costly drain on general revenues.

Both groups, in fact, were saying that they preferred features of the present system over the double-decker approach. The earnings-related feature of the present system was seen as a strength, both by those who wanted to maintain its adequacy elements and by those who wanted to retain the fiscal discipline which they believed that payroll tax financing imposed.

Women's groups also did not coalesce behind the double-decker option outlined in the report, largely because it did not equalize benefits between husbands and wives. Because the double-decker scheme failed to attract a constituency, attention continued to be centered on the earnings-sharing approach.

Earnings Sharing. Under earnings sharing, husbands' and wives' earnings for the years that they were married would be combined; each partner would then receive a benefit based on half the couple's combined earnings credits plus any earnings from before or after the marriage. The plan outlined in the 1979 HEW report proposed raising benefits for widows by providing a form of inherited credits—that is, by permitting a survivor to receive a benefit based on his or her own lifetime earnings, plus the deceased spouse's earnings from the years of marriage. Spouse's and survivors' benefits as paid under present law would be eliminated. The plan provided for the same reform principles as had the double-decker plan. In addition, it applied earnings sharing to married couples, thereby equalizing benefits between husbands and wives and avoiding the unequal treatment between married and divorced people that some found to be a problem with the double-decker plan.

Advisory Council and pension commission deliberations. A modification of earnings sharing was endorsed in concept by the 1979 Advisory Council on Social Security. Earnings sharing looked quite appealing because it met virtually all of the criteria about who should be treated alike. The President's Commission on Pension Policy was also attracted by the philosophical appeal of earnings sharing, and in its first interim report the commission endorsed the concept.[19] When the groups actually began to consider how earnings sharing would affect the distribution of benefits, however, some members began to have misgivings.

Perhaps the biggest stumbling block for the Advisory Council was the plan's effect on one-earner couples. The plan, by design, lowered benefits for one-earner couples to the level paid to two-earner couples with the same combined earnings. Analyses prepared for the council based on microsimulation projections showed that one-third of all couples would receive at least 5 percent less under earnings sharing than they would under present law and that 15 percent would receive at least 10 percent less than under present law. [20] Many council members, while endorsing the concept of equal benefits for couples with equal earnings, were not willing to achieve this at the expense of reducing benefits for the traditional family. They also were concerned about other groups of beneficiaries who would receive less under earnings sharing than under present law. These include, for example, divorced men and their subsequent families, who would receive lower benefits because earnings would have been shared with an ex-spouse. Also affected would be benefits for survivors of short marriages, who would inherit only for the years of marriage, rather than receiving benefits based on the deceased's entire earnings history.[21]

The Advisory Council also questioned whether the principles that earnings sharing incorporated did, in fact, represent a genuine consensus of American society: "The Council believes that it is important that the change reflect the views not only of those who are vocal, but also of the preponderance of those who would be affected by the application to Social Security of a view of the marital partnership that breaks with tradition." In particular, the council was concerned about mandating a transfer of benefits from husbands to wives, about eliminating protection for nonworking wives, and about providing benefits when no labor force earnings are lost. "Broad support of such fundamental change [in the Social Security system] is essential to its success," the report concluded.[22]

Unconvinced that such full support did exist for a full-scale earnings sharing plan that applied to both married and divorced couples, the council retreated from its earlier support for the concept. Many council members, however, believed that the benefits of divorced women and widows could be raised through a limited form of earnings sharing. A narrow majority (seven of thirteen members) therefore did endorse

- implementing earnings sharing at divorce for purposes of calculating retirement benefits (the provision would be mandatory only if one spouse applied for it)
- permitting inheritance of credits by widows and widowers
- phasing out spouse's and survivors' benefits for divorced and widowed persons[23]

The President's Commission on Pension Policy followed a similar course. In its final report, the commission endorsed the limited plan recommended earlier by the Advisory Council majority.[24]

Subsequent analyses. Shortly after the council reported to Congress, the Social Security Administration (SSA) staff developed further the council's interim proposals and the effects of their application. The group found that all the objectives that the council had hoped to achieve with earnings sharing at divorce and inheritance could not be realized because the objectives were not "fully compatible." The staff working paper notes: "In some cases, internal conflicts arise between the philosophy of the Council's plan and its goals about the distribution of benefits. In some other cases, conflicts occur between principles on which the plan is based and principles of the current Social Security program or of a sound transition plan."[25]

With regard to aged survivors, the group found that, despite being able to receive benefits based on both their own and their deceased spouse's earnings, some widows and widowers would receive lower benefits than under present law if existing survivors' benefits were phased out. The inherited credits would not be an exact substitute for present survivors' benefits. This is reflected in the cost estimates for the various proposals. The inherited-credit plan recommended by the Advisory Council was estimated to have a long-range average cost of 0.07 percent of taxable payroll. Further analyses revealed that the cost would rise to 0.23 percent of taxable payroll if survivors were to be assured they would not get lower benefits than under present law.[26] To eliminate so-called dependents' benefits for survivors by granting them "independent" credits would erode some of the protections for aged widows that had been provided through successive amendments over the years.

In practice earnings sharing would also make apparent a hard truth with regard to divorced women. Because it did not seem feasible to apply the new earnings sharing principle to divorces that had already occurred, the entire target group of today's older divorced women could not benefit from the earnings sharing approach.

Even if earnings sharing were applied only prospectively—that is, to future divorces only—there was a question about which years' earnings should be split. Some argued that it would be unfair to split earnings for years of marriage prior to enactment of the new principle. In this case, earnings sharing would fail to address the concerns not only of today's older divorced women but also of the cohorts following closely behind them. Today's older women who had had large families and low labor force participation rates during the post–World War II baby boom would not be helped by such a plan. Instead, it would be fully implemented only thirty to forty years from now for today's young women, whose higher employment rates and smaller families indicate that the problem will be of a different order of magnitude for them.

New equity dilemmas. The Advisory Council's deliberations and subsequent staff analysis by the SSA clarified the inherent conflict between either full-scale or limited earnings sharing and the individual earnings replacement principle that is integral to present law. The conflict is not as obvious when the analyses focus on couples in which both members are beneficiaries or in which both are not. The conflict becomes clear, however, when we consider couples in which only one member is retired or disabled. Under present law, the earnings replacement principle dictates that the benefit paid should be related to the lost earnings of the disabled or retired member. Earnings sharing, in contrast, dictates that the benefit should be based on half the couple's prior earnings regardless of whether all, some fraction, or none of the couple's earnings were lost by the one member's disability or retirement.

Earnings sharing, then, would significantly reduce benefits if the primary earner was disabled or retired. It would significantly increase benefits (or pay benefits where none are now paid) if the secondary earner (or homemaker) was disabled or retired. This redistribution—smaller benefits when more earnings are lost and more benefits when smaller or no earnings are lost—would be difficult to justify on the grounds of either earnings replacement or income adequacy. If actually implemented, it would probably seem unfair to many.

Further, present law ensures that a worker will never become worse off under social security by marrying or divorcing. Under earnings sharing, the worker's individual protection could be reduced by marriage or divorce because earnings credits would have been permanently transferred to a spouse.

Finally, the limited approach that applied earnings sharing to divorced people, but not to married people, obviously did not achieve the principle of treating alike married and divorced persons in otherwise similar circumstances. If benefits are to be increased for divorced women at the expense of their former husbands, but benefits for married couples are not to be affected, there is no way to avoid a so-called divorce bonus or a divorce penalty. This is particularly a problem when only one member of a couple is retired or disabled.

To summarize, then, the debate about family benefit issues in the 1970s emphasized new philosophical principles about who should be treated alike, rather than the particular changes in relative or absolute benefit levels that various constituencies wanted to achieve. The apparent agreement on principles led to support for earnings sharing as a comprehensive reform proposal. In some cases, the apparent agreement on principles masked basic disagreements over the desired results—particularly with regard to one- and two-earner couples. Some wanted to lower benefits for one-earner couples whereas others did not. Some wished to improve the position of working wives relative to homemakers; others did not. Some wanted to accord independent earnings credits to home-makers, but others were troubled by the consequences of doing so. In other cases there seemed to be fairly widespread agreement on the desired results: to raise benefits for divorced women and for survivors of dual-earner couples without lowering benefits for other widows. It was found, however, that these results were not achieved by either a comprehensive or a limited earnings sharing plan. Further, integral features of the present system—such as the relationship between benefit levels and earnings loss for individual workers—would be sacrificed in implementing the new principles.

Incremental Approaches to Changing Social Security

Reporting a year after the 1979 Advisory Council completed its work and several months after completion of the SSA staff's analysis, the National Commission on Social Security rejected both full-scale earnings sharing and the council's limited options. The commission report argued that it is "important to retain the earnings replacement principle on which the present program is based." [27] In explaining its dissatisfaction with the Advisory Council's limited options, the commission report cited the subsequent staff analysis, saying it considered "most serious . . . the evidence that the plan would lower benefits for a significant number of future beneficiaries, even for some whom the plan was designed to help." [28] Instead, the commission recommended what it considered to be cost-conscious ways to target limited benefit increases where they were most needed. The modest benefit increase in this area was part of a package that would result in a net reduction in the long-range cost of the system.

Low Benefits for Women. The commission recommended a change in the special minimum benefit to raise to the poverty threshold benefits of women who had had fairly long careers at low wages and past gaps in their careers because of child care responsibilities. The present special minimum benefit is based on a worker's number of years of coverage rather than on the AIME. It is paid only if it is higher than the regular AIME-based benefit. As of June 1981, the special monthly benefit is $16.07 per year of coverage for up to twenty years in excess of the first ten years. For a person with thirty years of coverage, it is $321. For a year to count toward the special minimum the worker must have earned at least a specified amount in that year—the amount now is $5,550, or about 40 percent of the average wage, or just under the federal minimum wage for a person who works full time all year.[29]

The commission's proposal would raise the number of countable years from twenty to twenty-five, thereby raising the upper limit on the special minimum to $402. It would also allow up to ten child care years to count as years of coverage. A child care year would be one in which the person had a child under age seven and did not otherwise earn enough for a year of coverage.

The proposal was estimated to have a long-range average cost of 0.14 percent of taxable payroll and was estimated to raise benefits of about 20 percent of retired women and 5 percent of retired men. All of those affected would, by definition, have had current benefits of less than $402 and would have been low earners with fairly long work records.

This approach has the potential for raising benefits for divorced women, a primary impetus for earnings sharing at divorce. It would do so, however, by taking account of the reason why many divorced women have low benefits in their own right, rather than taking account of divorce per se. Consequently, it would avoid new problems that would arise with proposals that attempt to treat divorced people differently from married people in otherwise similar circumstances. Indeed, it would also raise benefits for some working wives who had, in the past, been home-makers.[30]

Others have also recommended changes in the special minimum benefit. The special minimum, for example, could be made available to more persons if the earnings level that permits a year to be counted were reduced. The Subcommittee on the Treatment of Men and Women of the 1975 Advisory Council proposed that the amount of annual earnings needed to count as a year of coverage be lowered, arguing that this would aid all women who had worked regularly at low wages.[31] The change that it recommended would today lower the earnings requirement to about 27 percent of the average wage, or $3,700. This change could be implemented by itself, or be coupled with an increase in the number of years countable toward the special minimum.

To increase benefits for all regular low-wage earners, the 1979 Advisory Council recommended that the special minimum be raised—both by increasing the additional benefit associated with a year of coverage and by reducing the amount of earnings a worker must have had to be credited with a year of coverage.[32]

The child care credit plan recommended by the National Commission would apply only to the special minimum. From time to time, proposals have been made to permit child care years to be dropped from the regular benefit calculation, as is done in several foreign countries. Because of the high cost of child care dropout years, the 1979

Advisory Council recommended only that they be given "serious consideration at some future date."[33] Even the most restrictive version of the option—to permit a parent one additional dropout year per child if earnings were less than the amount needed for four quarters of coverage ($1,240 in 1981)—would have a long-range average cost of 0.20 percent of payroll.[34] The National Commission also rejected the notion or concept of child care dropout years because of their cost and target inefficiency. The National Commission noted that its approach not only was more directed toward those with low earnings, but also avoided some of the thorny issues of fairness that would arise in defining a child care dropout year.[35]

Each of these approaches could work within the current framework of social security. In doing so, they would also address a specific concern: low benefits because of child care years and/or very low wages. They do not, however, affect the disparity in benefits paid to one- and two-earner couples.

One- and Two-Earner Couples. The actions of these recent advisory groups (the 1979 Advisory Council on Social Security, the President's Commission on Pension Policy, and the National Commission on Social Security) suggest that the current disparity in benefits between one- and two-earner couples with the same combined earnings is not an issue of universal concern—or at least not of sufficient concern to persuade them to recommend lowering benefits for one-earner couples. It could also be argued that recent changes in the federal income tax structure support the retention of the somewhat higher benefits for one-earner couples.

The federal income tax system uses couples' income as the tax base. Couples with the same income generally have paid the same taxes. The 1981 change in the tax law modified this. Although the income tax system still uses couples' income as the tax base, one-earner couples and two-earner couples are no longer treated alike. One-earner couples pay somewhat more. The working spouse's deduction for two-earner couples is, in a way, similar to a homemaker tax for one-earner couples. If one-earner couples are subject to a "homemaker tax" under the federal tax system, one could now argue that there is some rough justice in providing a noncontributory old-age benefit to the homemaker spouse in the social security system and retaining the benefit inequality between one- and two-earner couples with the same combined earnings.

If, however, more nearly equal benefits for couples are desired, then it would be possible to move in that direction within the structure of the current system. We shall discuss first retirement benefits and then survivors' benefits.

TABLE 5

BENEFITS FOR A ONE-EARNER COUPLE AND A TWO-EARNER COUPLE
IF THE SPOUSE'S BENEFIT WERE 37.5 PERCENT OF PIA, 1981

	Couple's Combined Monthly Benefits ($)	
Couple's Combined Average Indexed Monthly Earnings ($)	One-earner couple (137.5% PIA)	Two-earner couple (each spouse earned half of combined AIME)
400	344	360
600	430	437
800	518	501
1,000	606	565
1,200	693	629
1,340	742	673

NOTE: The table shows full benefit amounts for workers. The cost-of-living adjustment of June 1981 is not reflected in these figures.
SOURCE: Authors' calculations.

Retirement benefits. Proposals to equalize retirement benefits between one- and two-earner couples usually take the form of leveling down because leveling up is prohibitively expensive.

Reducing the spouse's benefit amount payable at age sixty-five to 37.5 percent of the PIA (and to about 28 percent at age sixty-two) would result in more nearly equal benefits between one- and two-earner couples with the same earnings, as shown in table 5. This would reduce the long-range average cost by about 0.16 percent of payroll.[36]

A less severe approach would be to pay a spouse's benefit of 37.5 percent regardless of whether the benefit is claimed at age sixty-two or later. Because many wives now receive reduced spouse's benefits anyway, this approach would represent a smaller reduction for one-earner couples. In 1977, some 78 percent of wife beneficiaries were awarded reduced benefits before age sixty-five. This approach would narrow the difference between benefits for one- and two-earner couples, as shown in table 5. It also would save less—only 0.07 percent of payroll. This approach was considered by the National Commission, but was rejected because its members did not want to reduce benefits for those who claimed spouse's benefits after age sixty-two.[37]

Survivors' benefits. If the main problem with survivors' benefits is considered to be that survivors of low-earning dual-earner couples do not get enough relative to one-earner couples, then modest changes could be made to mitigate this dissatisfaction. Survivors of dual-earner couples could be permitted to receive some portion of the benefit based on their combined earnings, for example. All such proposals, of course, would represent a cost increase. The portion of the benefit and the earnings that could be combined would determine the cost and the types of dual-earner couples whose survivors' benefits would be increased.

Financial constraints clearly limit consideration of changes in the social security program that would increase its cost. In the income tax system, it is far easier to mitigate dissatisfaction about the treatment of one group relative to another at a time when overall tax rates are being lowered. Similarly, it is far easier to mitigate dissatisfaction with social security benefits at a time when benefits are being raised overall.

If the issues should be addressed, the experience of the past decade seems to argue for an incremental approach. Comprehensive approaches by definition affect more parts of the system than incremental approaches and are therefore more likely to create new inequities and to conflict with aspects of the present system that are integral to its acceptance. Further, comprehensive approaches sometimes serve simply to mask disparate views, rather than to represent genuine consensus about the desired direction of benefit changes. Incremental change can be directed more specifically to address particular problems. It can be scaled to the available financial resources, and it can be implemented in ways to minimize unintended side effects.

Notes

1. The payroll tax to finance Hospital Insurance (HI) under Medicare for the aged and disabled brings the total rate to 6.65 percent for employees and employers each. The self-employment tax rate is 8.00 percent for cash benefits and 9.30 percent including HI.

2. In 1981, annual benefits were offset by $1 for each $2 in annual earnings above $5,500 for those aged sixty-five to seventy-one. For those under sixty-five, benefits were offset by $1 for each $2 in earnings above $4,080. At age seventy-two or older, benefits are paid regardless of earnings.

3. For workers who reached age sixty-two in 1981 or became disabled or died (PIA is calculated for the deceased, and the survivor's benefit is based on that PIA) before age sixty-two in 1981, the formula is 90 percent of the first $211 of AIME, plus 32 percent of the next $1,063, plus 15 percent of AIME over $1,274. The percentages in the formula remain constant, but the dollar amounts, or bend points, rise each year for successive cohorts of new retirees by the change in average wages.

4. Retirement benefits are reduced by 20 percent if claimed at age sixty-two. Benefits are increased by rises in the cost of living after age sixty-two.

These adjustments are not shown in table 1.

5. The special minimum benefit is described in more detail in the section on incremental approaches to social security.

6. Monthly benefits under the 1935 act were based on accumulated covered earnings under the following formula: 1/2 of 1 percent of the first $3,000 in accumulated covered earnings, plus 1/12 of 1 percent of the next $42,000, plus 1/24 of 1 percent of the next $84,000. Under the 1939 act, monthly benefits were based on average taxable earnings and, according to the following formula, were 40 percent of the first $50 in average monthly earnings, plus 10 percent of the next $200. The resulting benefit was then increased by 1 percent for each year the worker had covered earnings of at least $200 under the system.

7. Senate Advisory Council on Social Security, *Final Report*, December 10, 1938, S. Doc. 4, 76th Cong., 1st sess., 1939, p. 15.

8. House Committee on Ways and Means, *Report of the Committee on Ways and Means on the Social Security Amendments of 1939*, H. Rept. 728, 76th Cong., 1st sess., June 2, 1939, p. 11.

9. Unpublished data from the Office of the Actuary, Social Security Administration, based on assumptions in the *1981 Annual Report of the Board of Trustees of the Federal Old-Age, Survivors and Disability Insurance Trust Funds* (Washington, D.C.: Social Security Administration, 1981). Alternative II-B assumptions are used.

10. Under present law, benefits for homemakers are based on present or former marital status, not on a test of dependency. Because the benefits are based on a spouse's work record, however, they are sometimes perceived to imply a "dependent" status.

11. President's Commission on the Status of Women, *Report of the Committee on Social Security and Taxes* (Washington, D.C., 1963), pp. 36 and 37.

12. Ibid., p. 37.

13. Citizens' Advisory Council on the Status of Women, *Report of the Task Force on Social Insurance and Taxes* (Washington, D.C., 1968), p. 72.

14. Ibid., p. 76.

15. Ibid., p. 73.

16. Department of State, National Commission on the Observance of International Women's Year, *"To Form a More Perfect Union": Justice of American Women* (Washington, D.C., 1968), p. 225.

17. Department of State, National Women's Conference, *Proposed National Plan of Action* (Washington, D.C., 1977), p. 18.

18. Department of Health, Education, and Welfare, *Social Security and the Changing Roles of Men and Women* (Washington, D.C., 1979).

19. President's Commission on Pension Policy, *An Interim Report* (Washington, D.C., May 1980), p. 30.

20. 1979 Advisory Council on Social Security, *Social Security Financing and Benefits: Report of the 1979 Advisory Council* (Washington, D.C.: Social Security Administration, 1982), p. 345.

21. Ibid., pp. 100–103.

22. Ibid., pp. 102 and 103.

23. Ibid., p. 103.

24. President's Commission on Pension Policy, *Coming of Age: Toward a National Retirement Policy* (Washington, D.C., 1981), p. 48.

25. Department of Health, Education, and Welfare, Social Security Administration, *Development of the Advisory Council's Interim Recommendations on the Treatment of Women*, Office of Policy Working Paper, September 12, 1980, p. 8.

26. Unpublished data from the Office of the Actuary, Social Security Administration.

27. National Commission on Social Security, *Social Security in America's Future: Final Report of the National Commission on Social Security, March, 1981* (Washington, D.C., 1981), p. 225.

28. Ibid., pp. 229–30.

29. Prior to 1978, the amount needed for a year of coverage toward the special minimum was equal to 25 percent of the maximum taxable earnings. When the ad hoc increases in the maximum were enacted in 1977, the amount needed for a year of coverage became 25 percent of what the taxable maximum would have been without the ad hoc increases.

30. The commission also recommended a plan for dividing a retired couple's benefit equally between spouses if either spouse chose to have benefits paid in separate checks.

31. House of Representatives, *Reports of the Quadrennial Advisory Council on Social Security*, H. Doc. 94-75, 94th Cong., 1st sess., 1975, pp. 147–48.

32. 1979 Advisory Council on Social Security, *Social Security Financing and Benefits*, p. 59.

33. Ibid., p. 108.

34. Ibid.

35. National Commission on Social Security, *Final Report*, pp. 236, 238.

36. Unpublished data from the Office of the Actuary, Social Security Administration.

37. The commission considered, but because of its high cost did not recommend, a working spouse's benefit plan that would produce more nearly equal benefits between one- and two-earner couples by paying a supplemental benefit to the lower-earning spouse in two-earner couples (National Commission on Social Security, *Final Report*, p. 231).

Commentary

Mickey Levy

The Reno-Upp paper provides a useful and well-organized summary of the treatment of women in social security and how that treatment evolved. The paper also clearly describes how different groups are treated under current policy and suggests criteria as guidelines for policy formation. Although Reno and Upp describe inadequacies in the current system and find fault with the earnings sharing approach, they do not make any recommendations. This ending leaves me dissatisfied. In addition, as a descriptive study, the paper lacks certain information that I would consider essential for policy making, and I find it misleading in several other regards.

There are three general obstacles to resolving the issue of the treatment of women in social security. First, the social security program includes cash payments for disability, as well as old-age and survivors' insurance. Each has its own eligibility requirements, and there are many rules that address different family structures. The Reno-Upp paper aptly reflects this complexity.

Second, social security is contributory, with individuals as the basis for payroll tax contributions and either the family or the individual as the basis for determining benefits, depending on the level of earnings and other characteristics of family members. The long-term nature of the program allows time for family composition to change, which complicates the issue of who the equals are. In addition, the program involves intragenerational transfers, which adds another dimension to the equity issue.

Third, Congress and others treat social security more like a religion than a public policy, and they would be hesitant to consider any change in the system, regardless of its conceptual appeal, if it reduced benefits to any group of recipients, such as married women, whether those recipients work or not. Any policy that would help some but not harm others would be costly. Since Congress is aware of the financial problems of the system, the total cost implications of any proposal are an obstacle to meaningful reform.

165

Given these obstacles or complexities, I would like to make the following comments. The first is very general. The complexity of the social security system breeds bad and still more complex policy. The system now tries to accomplish too much. A conceptually clean and legally defensible approach such as earnings sharing should not be rejected just because it does not address the problems incurred by every last individual in the system. In this regard, I would like to see more data analysis of beneficiaries under current law and under alternative proposals. Reno and Upp put great emphasis on winners and losers under various social security schemes without quantifying how many of them there would be and the magnitude of the gains and losses. These figures would be very important in determining the size of the "unintended consequences of possible alternatives." I believe that it is important to recognize complexity, but the existence of complexity should not paralyze us when making policy.

In considering current law and in designing an alternative policy, the attribution of earnings and the calculation of earnings histories define who the equals are. Reno and Upp are careful to identify equity criteria. We should note, however, that who the equals are may be considered separately from choosing the shape of the marginal benefit structure. Therefore, compared with current law, an alternative way to calculate earnings histories may change the distribution of benefits, but need not change their total amount.

Reno and Upp also persist in the Social Security Administration's notion of replacement rates as an adequate measure in evaluating either equity or adequacy. As I have stated elsewhere, the emphasis instead should be on rates of return. Consider, for example, the misleading information provided by replacement rates in table 2 of their paper. First, there is no consideration of lifetime contributions and, second, there is no consideration of after-tax returns, which, in light of the large rise in marginal tax rates, have grown substantially.

Further, the authors do not consider the issue of changing the tax treatment of social security. Taxing benefits that exceed contributions (or, for that matter, allowing all payroll taxes to be deductible and fully taxing benefits) would reduce the inequities that exist between multiple-earner couples on the one hand and single-earner households and individual workers on the other. Although I am aware of the political unpopularity of changing the tax treatment, just think of all of the improvements it would make.

I have several other minor points. In discussing the earnings sharing approach, the authors do not consider what to do with multiple-earner couples when one spouse works in uncovered employment such as in the federal government. Consider a Washington example: one spouse is a highly paid civil servant, and the other is a low-paid worker in the private sector. Should the low-paid worker still have to share covered earnings, even if there is no reciprocity—that is, the sharing of government earnings between spouses (for the purpose of determining civil service benefits)? Also, the Reno-Upp distinction between comprehensive versus incremental change is not helpful, since large conceptual changes need not involve large dollar changes.

In conclusion, although the labor force participation rate of women will rise somewhat in the future, the increase will not be as rapid as in the past. As a result, the dilemma of women in social security will persist. I view the earnings sharing approach, or some variation of it, as fruitful. Although the Reno and Upp paper presents problems with this approach, I do not think that the problems the authors reveal are insurmountable. I shall leave that to the next commentator to tell why.

Richard V. Burkhauser

The Reno-Upp paper offers an excellent view of the public policy decision-making process as perceived by past advisory councils and by many policy makers within the Social Security Administration. As such, I think it very clearly shows the difference between their perception of the world and the world as it is. This difference is the result of three major changes that have developed over the past forty years, especially in the past couple of years, and that are not fully recognized in most social security policy debates.

The first is the tremendous change in the social and legal relationships between women and men inside and outside of marriage. The second is the tremendous change in the mix of government programs aimed at providing aid to poor people outside of the social security system. The third is that a social security policy goal summarized by Martha Derthick as "a little bit more is always a good thing; anything less is inconceivable" is just not very realistic in an era of shrinking government budgets.[1]

Let us turn more specifically to the Reno and Upp paper. Like other government tax policies discussed at this conference, the treatment of different kinds of families under social security regulations is not uniform. This has resulted in substantial criticism of the system with regard to its effect on the distribution of income within and across families. A secondary criticism, but nevertheless of some relevance, is the behavioral responses current social security rules generate within and across families. A final issue that significantly affects potential changes in these regulations is their effect on overall costs.

167

Within-Household Issues

The right to a social security benefit in old age is the most valuable asset of the great majority of families in the United States. As Reno and Upp discuss, under current social security rules a direct right to that asset is provided to the person on whose record the benefit is based. A benefit is also available to a spouse based on one-half the retired worker's benefit. The effect of such a system of property rights is that a spouse holds only a one-third right to total family social security pension benefits, whereas the worker holds the right to two-thirds of total family benefits. In fact, the rights of the spouse are further reduced, since she (he) has no vested right to even this one-third share until a marriage has lasted ten years and cannot begin to receive benefits until the worker has died or retired. This, and not the issue of a test of dependency that Reno and Upp discuss, is at the heart of the criticism by those who argue that the social security system places homemakers in a dependent role.

It is important to recognize that this treatment of within-household property rights is virtually unique to social security and is a total anomaly with respect to the current treatment of property income by state courts. In 1939, when the current dependent-spouse system of family benefits was established, common law states held that parties to a divorce would take the property in the name of each. As Peter Martin shows, today in forty-seven states equal or equitable division of all assets of a marriage is the rule upon divorce.[2] This parallels actual family behavior, where the joint ownership of most assets—business, home, car—is the rule rather than exception. The 1979 decision of the U.S. Supreme Court in *Hisquiendo* v. *Hisquiendo* ruled that California law dealing with the division of property of a marriage upon divorce could not be applied to the Railroad Retirement pension program.[3] This ruling, Martin believes, will force state courts to ignore social security completely when they divide the assets of a marriage.

A shift from the current dependent-spouse system, under which property rights flow from the individual earnings of workers within a marriage, to earnings sharing, under which the property rights to all assets in a marriage are jointly owned, would be a fundamental change in the way in which property rights within marriage are viewed for purposes of social security. This is not only a change advocated by the National Women's Conference to which Reno and Upp allude but also one that has long since occurred with respect to the holding of most property in marriage. It is a reform with regard to the division of property in case of divorce already on the books in all community property states, as well as in the great majority of common law states. The social security system stands virtually alone in its treatment of the family in this regard.

The 1979 Social Security Advisory Council's statement quoted by Reno and Upp, in which it was noted that "it is important that the change [to earnings sharing] reflect the views not only of those who are vocal, but also of the preponderance of those who would be affected by the application to Social Security of a view of the marital partnership that breaks with tradition," underscores how out of touch policy makers within the social security system are with this evolution in family relations over the past forty years both in fact and in law.

Across-Family Issues

In an actuarially fair system in which benefits are based strictly on taxes paid into the system, a move from a dependent-spouse system to an earnings sharing system would change within-household property rights but have no effect across families. In fact, social security is both an annuity and a redistribution system, and a change would affect families differently. Elsewhere I show that the net effect of ending the dependent-spouse benefit and replacing it with earnings sharing would have a small effect on overall costs, but would shift benefits away from families in which one spouse had little or no work history, to households in which both spouses worked.[4] The pattern of losses is similar to that found in the Advisory Council's study—a range of 5 to 10 percent.[5]

To a social security establishment whose policy prescription can be summed up as, "A little bit more is always a good thing; anything less is inconceivable," such losses in benefits may loom large.[6] To put it in perspective, however, had such a change been made in June of 1981, when social security benefits were automatically increased to adjust for inflation, the 11 percent increase would have guaranteed that no family would have received a smaller social security check. More important, with respect to the merits of such a policy change, who would have suffered from such a change?

Reno and Upp argue correctly that the original purpose of the spouse's benefit was to direct additional social security benefits in the early years of the system to families in greatest need, with a minimum increase in overall costs. Redistributing income to those with the greatest need at the least cost makes as much sense today as it did in 1939. Unfortunately, using a dependent-spouse system to achieve this goal in today's world makes much less sense.

As we have already argued, the social security establishment has been slow to recognize and adjust to changes in the role of women and men in society. It has been even slower in recognizing that Supplemental Security Income (SSI) now provides the most efficient mechanism for redistributing income to the elderly poor. The implementation in 1974

169

of this general-revenue-financed negative income tax system made many of the redistribution features of social security redundant. Ending the spouse's benefit would have no effect on the vast majority of low-income couples it was originally intended to help. Even before SSI, Holden argues, the spouse's benefit in fact was not very efficient.[7] This subsidy has historically provided more benefits to upper-income families than to lower-income families. The result is not too surprising since the spouse's benefit is based on the earnings record of the husband. The family of a higher-wage-earning husband receives a bigger spouse's benefit. In addition, in lower-income families both the husband and the wife are more likely to be working and to have closer earnings histories than husbands and wives in higher-income families. These are family characteristics that reduce the marginal subsidy provided by a spouse's benefit. As I show elsewhere, the major losers of the change to earnings sharing would be the families of high earners with a spouse who has no earnings record and not incidentally has never paid social security taxes.[8] The existence of SSI removes the early justification for a spouse's benefit as an efficient redistribution mechanism and makes it difficult to argue on the grounds of either efficiency or adequacy that we continue to need it for this purpose.

Behavioral Responses

Unlike the federal income tax, there is some relationship between social security payroll taxes and subsequent benefits. Because of this relationship, John Turner and I argued that the effect of this tax on behavior varies over the lifetime.[9] If we hold the nominal payroll tax rate constant, the net tax paid varies over the lifetime and is in fact a net subsidy to work at certain ages. The net tax paid varies to the degree that the expected value of future social security benefits changes with an increase in social-security-taxed wage earnings in a given period. The dependent-spouse system makes the social security payroll tax payments of many women redundant since they receive no additional benefits from it. Even for those whose earnings yield benefits in excess of those provided by a spouse's benefit, average yield from taxes paid is still low. This point is also made by O'Neill in this volume.

The fairness of such a system is open to question. Its impact on work behavior is not. Such a system induces married couples to specialize in either home or market work. This clearly is in opposition to the current trends in labor supply behavior where in one-half of all married couples, both the husband and the wife are in the work force at the same time. An increase in the net tax paid by a spouse who works is not necessarily a subsidy to child care, as some of the proponents of the dependent-spouse system argue, but rather to child care by one spouse, rather than a sharing of child care, housework, and market work by both spouses.

As we have seen before, however, even this subsidy to the "traditional family" is not without its dangers to women who accept the role of sole provider of child care. In the event of divorce before ten years of marriage, social security provides no protection to a spouse. This is not an insignificant risk given that today nearly one-half of first marriages end in divorce, with the majority breaking up before ten years. Such statistics emphasize the dangers even to those women in so-called traditional families for whom the current system is allegedly gearing protection. Earnings sharing would prevent this. It would cause both the husband and the wife to share the costs of child care and yield them equal returns from market work.

Fundamental versus Incremental Reform

Earnings sharing would fundamentally change the within-household property rights of a worker and spouse. In addition, it would incrementally change the across-family distribution of social security benefits. If earnings sharing replaced the dependent-spouse benefit, overall cost would not change, but families with two earners would gain slightly and some families with only one earner would lose moderately.

Reno and Upp argue that a change to earnings sharing is not incremental, since it would greatly affect earnings replacement rates, which are viewed as a crucial policy parameter in social security debates. Although this is true, it underscores the inability of a replacement rate to describe adequately the true value of social security benefits, rather than any significant change in the well-being of families caused by a shift to earnings sharing.

In its simplest form, a replacement rate shows the ratio of pre- and postretirement income. Even in its more sophisicated forms, its myopic concentration on income in a single year fails to take into account the life-cycle nature of social security benefits. Such a measure, for instance, would argue that a worker is better off to postpone acceptance of social security past age sixty-two, since for each year benefits are postponed replacement rates increase. Clearly most workers do not behave that way. Rather they consider the asset value of the full stream of social security benefits. They compare the value of a stream of smaller yearly benefits available now with a stream of larger yearly benefits available at a later date. They choose to take social security benefits at the age most valuable to them.

Earnings sharing will have some effect on the well-being of families

171

in which the husband and wife are of different ages, but comparing single-year replacement rates will not indicate the degree of change. This is not to say that such a change will not affect couples and their work behavior. Rather it argues, for instance, that in families where husbands are significantly older than their wives, they will either have to save more or the wife will have to work more to achieve the same level of income in the first years of retirement as would have occurred previously. To the degree that people are myopic or men and women cannot move in and out of the work force, then short-term variations may lead to liquidity problems.

Incremental reform in the final analysis is in the eye of the beholder. The proposals made by the National Commission on Social Security and its criticism of the limited recommendations made by the 1979 Advisory Council fail to recognize that the era of continuous social security growth is over. Additional benefits to some will come only at the expense of real reductions to others. The across-the-generation transfer that allowed all older workers to receive far more in benefits than they and their employers had paid for them in payroll taxes is no longer possible. This has already caused a closer scrutiny of the mechanisms for providing social security benefits. The National Commission's rejection of earnings sharing because of "the evidence that it would lower benefits for a significant number of future beneficiaries," as quoted by Reno and Upp, is no longer sufficient cause to reject such a change. Rather, we must ask whether the redistributive aspects of social security which do not direct additional benefits to those most in need at the lowest cost should be continued in an era when a little bit more is *not* always a good thing.

Discussion Summary

In responding to Mickey Levy and Richard Burkhauser, the authors noted that they did not oppose earnings sharing because of its effects on replacement rates. They felt that it would radically change the distribution of benefits, often in ways that would be considered inequitable. With earnings sharing, for example, the benefits to a family would be the same whether the primary worker or the homemaker became disabled. Many would say that the two cases should not be treated the same.

Replying to Burkhauser's point that Supplemental Security Income makes it much less important that social security serve a welfare role, it was noted that this notion is not universally accepted as evidenced by the heated 1981 political debate over elimination of the minimum benefit.

A member of the audience noted that it was odd that in discussing earnings sharing Reno and Upp placed great emphasis on need, but Levy and Burkhauser did not seem to think that social security had to take account of social need at all. Levy replied that he only wanted to stress the importance of looking at rates of return in after-tax dollars rather than replacement rates in assessing fairness. He did not want to rule out the possibility that rates of return would vary in a progressive manner. Burkhauser added that he did not believe that social security should be a pure insurance system. When we part from pure insurance principles, however, he felt that it should be done in a manner that reflects the needs of the beneficiaries. The major beneficiaries of dependents' benefits in today's world are relatively high-income, one-earner families, and that does not reflect need.

Joseph Pechman said that he wondered how the two discussants could, on the one hand, emphasize rates of return as a criterion for judging the benefit structure, but, on the other, favor earnings sharing over the double-decker approach, which accomplishes the same thing. Burkhauser replied that one could argue about the merits of a double-decker system with or without means testing, but he believed that the current benefit structure was already the equivalent of a double-decker system in that in the first benefit bracket 90 percent of the AIME is replaced. Pechman responded that with an implicit double-decker system, we could end the dependent spouse's benefit and thus take a big step toward the rate-of-return objective emphasized by Levy and Burkhauser.

Lawrence Thompson said earnings sharing should be considered a comprehensive change and not an incremental change. The difference between the two is not a question of how much money the plan would cost or save, nor of whether it achieved intended benefit changes between one- and two-earner couples. Earnings sharing would be a comprehensive change because it would permanently change earnings records for all married and formerly married persons. Their earnings records are the basis for many benefit calculations other than retired couples' benefits. Benefits for surviving children, widowed mothers and fathers, and disabled workers and their families would also be affected, unless special provision were made to override the effects of earnings sharing in such cases. Attempts to work through the unintended effects of earnings sharing force one to recognize the complexity of the current benefit structure and the comprehensiveness of any change that calls for reallocating earnings records between people.

Notes

1. Martha Derthick, *Policymaking for Social Security* (Washington, D.C.: Brookings Institution, 1979).

2. Peter W. Martin, "Comments on Earnings-Sharing and Universal Coverage," AEI Conference on Social Security, June 26, 1981.

3. *Hisquiendo* v. *Hisquiendo*, 439 U.S. 572 (1979).

4. Richard V. Burkhauser, "Alternative Social Security Responses to the Changing Roles of Women and Men," AEI Conference on Social Security, June 26, 1981.

5. *Report of the Quadrennial Advisory Council on Social Security*, 1979.

6. Derthick, *Policymaking for Social Security*.

7. Karen Holden, "Supplemental OASI Benefits to Homemakers through Current Spouse Benefits, a Homemaker's Credit, and Child-Care Dropout Years," in *The Changing Roles of Women and Men: A Challenge to the Social Security System*, ed. Richard V. Burkhauser and Karen Holden (New York: Academic Press, 1982).

8. Burkhauser, "Alternative Social Security Responses."

9. Richard Burkhauser and John Turner, "Can Twenty-five Million Americans Be Wrong?—A Response to Blinder, Gordon, and Wise," *National Tax Journal* (December 1981).

A Note on the Book

This book was edited by Donna Spitler
and by Claire Theune of the
Publications Staff of the American Enterprise Institute.
The staff also designed the cover and format, with Pat Taylor.
The figures were drawn by Hördur Karlsson.
The text was set in Times Roman, a typeface designed by
Stanley Morison. Hendricks-Miller Typographic Company,
of Washington, D.C., set the type, and BookCrafters of Chelsea,
Michigan, printed and bound the book, using paper made
by the P. H. Glatfelter Company.

SELECTED AEI PUBLICATIONS